ON THE

LESSONS IN PROVERBS.

ON THE

LESSONS IN PROVERBS

BEING THE SUBSTANCE OF

LECTURES DELIVERED TO YOUNG MEN'S SOCIETIES

AT PORTSMOUTH AND ELSEWHERE

BY

RICHARD CHENEVIX TRENCH, B. D.

AUTHOR OF "THE STUDY OF WORDS," "SYNONYMS OF THE NEW TESTAMENT," ETC.
VICAR OF ITCHENSTOKE, HANTS; EXAMINING CHAPLAIN TO THE LORD BISHOP
OF OXFORD; AND PROFESSOR OF DIVINITY, KING'S COLLEGE, LONDON.

FROM THE SECOND LONDON EDITION—REVISED AND ENLARGED

REDFIELD
110 AND 112 NASSAU STREET, NEW YORK.
Fourth Edition.]
1855.

PREFACE.

It may be as well to state that the lectures which are here published were never delivered as a complete course, but only one here and two there, as matter gradually grew under my hands; yet so that very much the greater part of what is contained in this volume has been at one time or another actually delivered. Although I have always taken a lively interest in national proverbs, I had no intention at the first of making a book about them; but only selected the subject as one which I thought—though I was not confident of this—might afford me sufficient material for a single lecture, which I had undertaken some time ago to deliver. I confess that I was at that time almost entirely ignorant of the immense number and variety of books bearing on the subject. Many of these I still know only by name. With some of the best, however, I have made myself acquainted; and by their aid, with the addition of such further material as I could myself furnish, these lectures have assumed their present shape: and I publish them because none of the works on proverbs which I know are exactly that book for all readers which I could have wished to see. Either they include matter which can not be fitly placed before all —or they address themselves to the scholar alone, or if not so, are at any rate inaccessible to the mere English reader—or they contain bare lists of proverbs, with no endeavor to compare, illustrate, and explain them—or if they do seek to explain, yet they do it without attempting to sound the depths or measure the real significance of that which they undertake to unfold. From these or other causes it has come to pass that with a multitude of books, many of them admirable, on a subject so popular, there is no single one which is frequent in the hands of men. I will not deny that, with all the slightness and shortcomings of my own, I have still hoped to supply, at least for the present, this deficiency.

ITCHENSTOKE, HANTS (ENGLAND).

CONTENTS.

ON

THE LESSONS IN PROVERBS.

LECTURE I.

THE FORM AND DEFINITION OF A PROVERB.

It may very easily have happened that from some of us proverbs have never attracted the notice which I am persuaded they deserve; and from this, it may follow that, when invited to bestow even a brief attention on them, we are in some doubt whether they will repay our pains. We think of them but as sayings on the lips of the multitude; not a few of them have been familiar to us as far back as we can remember; often employed by ourselves, or in our hearing, on slight and trivial occasions: and thus, from these and other causes, it may very well be, that, however sometimes one may have taken our fancy, we yet have remained blind in the main to the wit, wisdom, and imagination, of which they are full; and very little conscious of the amusement, instruction, insight, which they are capable of yielding. Unless too we have devoted a certain attention to the subject, we may not be at all aware how little those more familiar ones, which are frequent on the lips of men, exhaust the treasure of our native proverbs; how many and what excellent ones remain behind, having now for the most part fallen out of sight; or what riches in like kind other nations possess. We may little guess how many aspects of interest there are in which our own by themselves, and again our own compared with those of other people, may be regarded.

And yet there is much to induce us to reconsider our judgment, should we be thus tempted to slight them, and to count them not merely trite, but trivial and unworthy of a serious attention. The fact that they please the people, and have pleased them for ages—that they possess so vigorous a principle of life, as to have maintained their ground, ever new and ever young, through all the centuries of a nation's existence—nay, that many of them have pleased not one nation only, but many, so that they have made themselves a home in the most different lands—and further, that they have, not a few of them, come down to us from remotest antiquity, borne safely upon the waters of that great stream of time, which has swallowed so much beneath its waves—all this, I think, may well make us pause, should we be tempted to turn away from them with anything of indifference or disdain.

And then further, there is this to be considered, that some of the greatest poets, the profoundest philosophers, the most learned scholars, the most genial writers in every kind, have delighted in them, have made large and frequent use of them, have bestowed infinite labor on the gathering and elucidating of them. In a fastidious age, indeed, and one of false refinement, they may go nearly or quite out of use among the so-called upper classes. "No gentleman," says Lord Chesterfield, or "no man of fashion," as I think is his exact phrase, "ever uses a proverb."* And with how fine a touch of nature Shakespeare makes Coriolanus, the man who, with all his greatness, is entirely devoid of all sympathy for the people, to utter his scorn *of them* in scorn of their proverbs, and of their frequent employment of these:—

> "Hang 'em!
> They said they were an hungry, sighed forth proverbs;—
> That, *hunger broke stone walls;* that, *dogs must eat;*
> That, *meat was made for mouths;* that, *the gods sent not*
> *Corn for the rich men only;*—with these shreds
> They vented their complainings."
>
> *Coriolanus*, Act I. Sc. 1.

But that they have been always dear to the true intellectual aristocracy of a nation, there is abun-

* A similar contempt of them speaks out in the antithesis of the French Jesuit, Bouhours: "Les proverbes sont les sentences du peuple, et les sentences sont les proverbs des honnêtes gens."

dant evidence to prove. Take but these three names in evidence, which though few, are in themselves a host. Aristotle made a collection of proverbs; nor did he count that he was herein doing aught unworthy of his great reputation, however some of his adversaries may afterward have made of the fact that he did so a charge against him. He is said to have been the first collector of them, though many afterward followed in the same path. Shakespeare loves them so well, that besides often citing them, and scattering innumerable covert allusions, rapid side glances at them which we are in danger of missing unless at home in the proverbs of England, several of his plays, as *Measure for Measure*, *All's well that ends well*, have popular proverbs for their titles. And Cervantes, a name only inferior to Shakespeare, has made very plain the affection with which he regarded them. Every reader of *Don Quixote*, will remember his squire, who sometimes can not open his mouth but there drop from it almost as many proverbs as words. I might name others who have held the proverb in honor—men who though they may not attain to these first three, are yet deservedly accounted great; as Plautus, the most genial of Latin poets, Rabelais and Montaigne the two most original of French authors; and how often Fuller, whom Coleridge has styled the wittiest of writers, justifies this praise in his witty employment of some old proverb; and no reader can thoroughly understand and enjoy *Hudibras*, none but will miss a multitude of its keenest allusions, who is not thoroughly familiar with the proverbial literature of England.

Nor is this all; we may with reverence adduce quite another name than any of these, the Lord himself, as condescending to employ such proverbs as he found current among his people. Thus, on the occasion of his first open appearance in the synagogue of Nazareth, he refers to the proverb, *Physician heal thyself* (Luke iv. 23), as one which his hearers will perhaps bring forward against himself; and again personally to another, *A prophet is not without honor but in his own country*, as attested in his own history; and at the well of Sychar he declares, "Herein is that saying," or that proverb, "true, *One soweth, and another reapeth*" (John iv. 37). But he is much more than a quoter of other men's proverbs; he is a maker of his own. As all forms of human composition find their archetypes and their highest realization in Scripture, as there is no tragedy like Job, no pastoral like Ruth, no lyric melodies like the Psalms, so we should affirm no proverbs like those of Solomon, were it not that "a greater than Solomon" has drawn out of the rich treasure house of the Eternal Wisdom a series of proverbs more costly still. For indeed how much of our Lord's teaching, especially as recorded in the first three Evangelists, is thrown into this form; and how many of his words have in this shape passed over as "faithful sayings" upon the lips of men; and so doing have fulfilled a necessary condition of the proverb, whereof we shall have presently to speak.

But not urging this testimony any further—a testimony too august to be lightly used, or employed merely to swell the testimonies of men—least of all, men of such "uncircumcised lips" as, with all their genius, were more than one of these whom I have named—and appealing only to the latter, I shall be justified, I feel, in affirming that whether we listen to those single voices which make a silence for themselves, and are heard through the centuries and their ages, or to that great universal voice of humanity, which is wiser even than these, for it is these, with all else which is worthy to be heard added to them, there is here a subject, which those whose judgments should go very far with us have not accounted unworthy of their serious regard.

And I am sure if we bestow on them ourselves even a moderate share of attention, we shall be ready to set our own seal to the judgment of wiser men that have preceded us here. For, indeed, what a body of popular good sense and good feeling, as we shall then perceive, is contained in the better, which is also the more numerous portion of them; what a sense of natural equity, what a spirit of kindness breathes out from many of them; what prudent rules for the management of life, what shrewd wisdom, which though not *of* this world, is most truly *for* it, what frugality, what patience, what perseverance, what manly independence, are continually inculcated by them. What a fine knowledge of the human heart do many of them display; what useful, and not always obvious, hints do they offer on most important points, as on the choice of companions, the bringing up of children, the bearing of prosperity and adversity, the restraint of all immoderate expectations. And they take a yet higher range than this; they have their ethics, their theology, their views of man in his highest relations of all, as a man with his fellow-man, and man with his Maker. Be these always correct or not, and I should be very far from affirming that they always are so, the student of humanity, he who because he is a man counts nothing human to be alien to him, can never without wilfully foregoing an important document, and one which would have helped him often in his studies, altogether neglect or pass them by.

But what, it may be asked before we proceed further, is a proverb? Nothing is harder than a definition. While on the one hand there is for the most part no easier task than to detect a fault or flaw in the definition of those who have gone before us, nothing on the other is more difficult than to propose one of our own, which shall not also present a vulnerable side. Some one has said that these three things go to the constituting of a proverb, *shortness, sense, and salt.* In brief, pointed sayings of this kind, the second of the qualities enumerated here, namely, *sense*, is sometimes sacrificed to alliteration. I would not affirm that it is so here: for the words are not ill-spoken, though they are very far from satisfying the rigorous requirements of a definition, as will be seen when we consider what the writer intended by his three *esses*, which it is not hard to understand. The proverb, he would say, must have *shortness;* it must be succinct, utterable in a breath. It must have *sense*, not being that is, the mere small talk of conversation, slight and trivial, else it would perish as soon as born, no one taking the trouble to keep it alive. It must have *salt*, that is, besides its good sense, it must in its manner and outward form being pointed and pungent, having a sting in it, a barb which shall not suffer it to drop lightly from the memory.*

Yet, regarded as a definition, this of the triple *s*

* Compare with this Martial's so happy epigram upon epigrams, in which everything runs exactly parallel to that which has been said above:—

> "Omne epigramma sit instar apis; sit aculeus illi,
> Sint sua mella, sit et corporis exigui;"

which may be indifferently rendered thus:—

> Three things must epigrams, like bees, have all—
> A sting, and honey, and a body small.

fails, as I have said; it indeed errs in both defect and excess.

Thus, in demanding *shortness*, it errs in excess. It is, indeed, quite certain that a good proverb will be short—as short, that is, as is compatible with the full and forcible conveying of that which it intends. Brevity, "the soul of wit," will be eminently the soul of a proverb's wit. Oftentimes it will consist of two, three, or four, and these sometimes monosyllabic words. Thus: *Extremes meet;*—*Right wrongs no man;*—*Forewarned, forearmed;*—with a thousand more.* But still, shortness is only a relative term, and it would, perhaps, be more accurate to say that a proverb must be *concise*—cut down, that is, to the fewest possible words; condensed, quintessential wisdom.† But that, if only it fulfil this condition of being as short as possible, it need not be absolutely very short, there are sufficient examples to prove. Thus, Freytag has admitted the following, which indeed hovers on the confines of the fable, into his great collection of Arabic

* The very shortest proverb which I know in the world is this German: "Voll, toll;" which sets out very well the connection between fullness and folly, pride and abundance of bread. In that seeking of extreme brevity noted above, they sometimes become exceedingly elliptical (although this is the case more with the ancient than with the modern), so much so as to omit even the vital element of the sentence, the verb. Thus: Χρήματ' ἀνήρ: "Sus Minervam;" "Fures clamorem;" "Meretrix pudicam;" "Amantes amentes."

† This is what Aristotle means when he ascribes συντομία—which in another place he opposes to the ὄγκος λέξεως—to it.

proverbs: "*They said to the camel-bird* [*i.e.*, the ostrich], '*Carry;*' *it answered*, '*I can not, for I am a bird.*' *They said* '*Fly;*' *it answered*, '*I can not, for I am a camel.*'" This could not be shorter, yet, as compared with the greater number of proverbs, is not short.* Even so the *sense* and *salt*, which are ascribed to the proverb as other of its necessary conditions, can hardly be said to be such; seeing that flat, saltless proverbs, though comparatively rare, they certainly are; while yet, be it remembered, we are not considering now what are the ornaments of a *good* proverb, but the essential marks of all.

And then, moreover, it errs in defect; it has plainly omitted one quality of the proverb, and that the most essential of all—I mean *popularity;* acceptance and adoption on the part of the people. Without this popularity, without these suffrages and this consent of the many, no saying, however brief, however wise, however seasoned with salt, however worthy on all these accounts to have become a proverb, however fulfilling all other its conditions, can yet be esteemed as such. This popularity, omitted

* Let serve for further proof this eminently witty old German proverb, which, despite its apparent length, has not forfeited its character as such. I shall prefer to leave it in the original: "Man spricht, an viererlei Leuten ist Mangel auf Erden: an Pfaffen, sonst dürfte einer nit 6 bis 7 Pfruenden; an Adelichen, sonst wollte nit jeder Bauer ein Junker sein; an Huren, sonst würden die Handwerk Eheweiber und Nunnen nit treiben; an Juden, sonst würden Christen nit wuchern."

in that enumeration of the essential notes of the proverb, is yet the only one whose presence is absolutely necessary, whose absence is fatal to the claims of any saying to be regarded as such.

Those, however, who have occupied themselves with the making of collections of proverbs have sometimes failed to realize this to themselves with sufficient clearness, or, at any rate, have not kept it always before them; and thus it has come to pass, that many collections include whatever brief sayings their gatherers have anywhere met with, which to them have appeared keenly, or wisely, or wittily spoken;* while yet a multitude of these have never received their adoption into the great family of proverbs, or their rights of citizenship therein: inasmuch as they have never passed into general recognition and currency, have no claim to this title, however just a claim they may have on other grounds to our admiration and honor. For instance, this word of Goethe's, "A man need not be an architect to live in a house," seems to me

* When Erasmus, after discussing and rejecting the definitions of those who had gone before him, himself defines the proverb thus, "Celebre dictum, scitâ quà piam novitate, insigne," it appears to me that he has not escaped the fault which he has blamed in others—that, namely, of confounding the accidental adjuncts of a *good* proverb, with the necessary conditions of *every* proverb. In rigor, the whole second clause of the definition should be dismissed, and *Celebre dictum* alone remain. Better Eifelein (*Sprichwörter des Deutschen Volkes*, Friburg, 1840, p. x.): "Das sprichwort ist ein mit öffentlichen Gepaäge ausgemünzter Saz, der seinen Curs und anerkannten Werth under dem Volke hat."

to have every essential of a proverb, saving only that it has not passed over upon the lips of men. It is a saying of manifold application; a universal law is knit up in a particular example: I mean that gracious law in the distribution of blessing, which does not limit our use and enjoyment of things by our understanding of them, but continually makes the enjoyment much wider than the knowledge; so that it is not required that one be a botanist to have pleasure in a rose, nor a critic to delight in *Paradise Lost*, nor a theologian to taste all the blessings of Christian faith, nor, as he expresses it, an architect to live in a house. And here is an inimitable saying of Schiller's: "Heaven and earth fight in vain against a dunce;" yet it is not a proverb, because his alone; although abundantly worthy to have become such,* moving as it does in the same line with, though far superior to, the Chinese proverb, which itself also is good: *One has never so much need of his wit, as when he has to do with a fool.*

Or, to take another example still more to the point. James Howell, a prolific English writer of the seventeenth century, one certainly meriting better than that almost entire oblivion into which his writings have fallen, occupied himself much with proverbs, and, besides collecting those of oth-

* It suggests, however, the admirable Spanish proverb, spoken, no doubt, out of the same conviction: "Dios me dè contienda, con quien me entienda."

ers, has, himself set down "five hundred new sayings, which, in tract of time may serve for proverbs to posterity." As was to be expected, they have not so done; for it is not after this artificial method that such are born; yet many of these proverbs in expectation are expressed with sense and felicity; for example: "Pride is a flower that grows in the devil's garden;" as again, the selfishness which characterizes too many of them is not ill reproduced in the following: "Burn not thy fingers to snuff another man's candle;" and there is, at any rate, good theology in the following: "Faith is a great lady, and good works are her attendants." Yet, for all this, it would be inaccurate to quote these as proverbs (and their author himself, as we have seen, did not do more than set them out as proverbs upon trial), inasmuch as they have remained the private property of him who first devised them, never having passed into general circulation; which until men's sayings have done, maxims, sentences, apothegms, aphorisms, they may be, and these of excellent temper and proof; but proverbs, as yet, they are not.

It is because of this, the popularity inherent in a genuine proverb, that from such a one, in a certain sense, there is no appeal. You will not suppose me to intend that there is no appeal from its wisdom, truth, or justice; from any word of man's there may be such, but no appeal from it as most truly representing a popular conviction. Aristotle, who in his ethical and political writings often finds very much more, always finds this in it. It may not be, it very often will not be, a universal conviction which it expresses, but ever one popular and widespread. So far indeed from a universal, very often, over against the one proverb there will be another, its direct antagonist; and the one shall belong to the kingdom of light, the other to the kingdom of darkness. "*Common fame is seldom to blame:*" here is the baser proverb, for as many as drink in with greedy ears all reports to the injury of their neighbors, being determined from the first that they *shall* be true. But it is not left without its compensation: "'*They say so' is half a liar:*" here is the better word with which *they* may arm themselves, who count it a primal duty to close their ears against all such unauthenticated rumors to the discredit of their brethren. "*The noblest vengeance is to forgive:*" here is the godlike proverb on the manner in which wrongs should be recompensed: "*He who can not revenge himself is weak, he who will not is vile:*"* here is the devilish. There are some lines of an old English poet in praise of proverbs:—

"The people's voice the voice of God we call;
And what are proverbs but the people's voice?
Coined first, and current made by public choice—
Then sure they must have weight and truth withal."

* "Chi non può fare sua vendetta è debile, chi non vuole è vile."

It will follow, from what has just been said, that these, true in the main, will yet require to be taken with certain qualifications and exceptions.*

Herein, in great part, the force of a proverb lies, namely that it has already received the stamp of popular allowance. A man might produce (for what another has done he might do again) something as witty, as forcible, as much to the point, of his own; which should be hammered at the instant on his own anvil. Yet still it is not "the wisdom of many;" it has not stood the test of experience; it wants that which the other already has, but which it only after a long period can acquire—the consenting voice of many, and at different times, to its wisdom and truth. A man employing a long-recognised proverb is not speaking of his own, but uttering a faith and conviction very far wider than that of himself or of any single man; and it is because he is so doing that they, in Lord Bacon's words, "serve not only for ornament and delight, but also for active and civil use; as being the edge-tools of speech, which cut and penetrate the knots of business and affairs." The proverb has, in fact, the same advantage over the word now pro-

* Quintilian's words (*Inst.* 5, 11, 41), which are to the same effect, must be taken with the same exceptions: "Neque enim durâssent hæc in æternum, nisi vera omnibus viderentur;" and also Don Quixote's: "Parécеme me, Sancho, que no ay refrán que no sea verdadéro, porque todas son sentencias sacadas de la misma experiencia, madre de las ciencias todas."

duced for the first time, which, for present currency, and value, has the recognised coin of the realm over the rude unstamped ore newly washed from the stream, or dug up from the mine. This last *may* possess an equal amount of fineness; but the other has been stamped long ago as already passed often from man to man, and found free acceptance with all:* it inspires, therefore, a confidence which the ruder metal can not at present challenge. And the same satisfaction which the educated man finds in referring the particular matter before him to the universal law which rules it, a plainer man finds in the appeal to a proverb. He is doing the same thing; taking refuge, that is, as each man so gladly does, from his mere self and single fallible judgment, in a larger experience and in a wider conviction.

And in all this which has been urged lies, as it seems to me, the explanation of a sentence of an ancient grammarian, which at first sight appears to contain a bald absurdity, namely, that a proverb is "a saying without an author." For, however without a *known* author it may, and in the majority of cases it must be, still, as we no more believe in the spontaneous generation of proverbs than of anything else, an author every one of them must have

* Thus, in a proverb about proverbs, the Italians say, with a true insight into this its prerogative: "Il proverbio *s'invecchia*, e chi vuol far bene, vi si specchia."

had. It might, however, and it often will have been, that in its utterance the author did not *precipitate* the floating convictions of the society round him; he did but clothe in happier form what others had already felt, or even already uttered; for often a proverb has been in this aspect, "the wit of one and the wisdom of many." And further, its constitutive element, as we must all now perceive, is not the utterance on the part of the one, but the acceptance on the part of the many. It is *their* sanction which first makes it to be such; so that every one who took or gave it during the period when it was struggling into recognition may claim to have had a share in its production; and in this sense, without any single author it may have been. From the very first the people will have vindicated it for their own. And thus, though they do not always analyze the compliment paid to them in the use of their proverbs, they always feel it; they feel that a writer or speaker using these is putting himself on their ground, is entering on their religion, and they welcome him the more cordially for this.*

Let us now consider if some other have not sometimes been proposed as essential notes of the prov-

* The name which the proverb bears in Spanish points to this fact, that popularity is a necessary condition of it. This name is not *proverbio*, for that in Spanish signifies an apothegm, an aphorism, a maxim; but *refran*, which is *a referendo*, from the oftenness of its repetition. The etymology of the Greek παροιμία is somewhat doubtful, but it, too, means probably a trite, wayside saying.

2

erb, which yet are in fact accidents, such as may be present or absent without affecting it vitally. Into an error of this kind they have fallen, who have claimed for the proverb, and made it one of its necessary conditions that it should be a figurative expression. A moment's consideration will be sufficient to disprove this. How many proverbs, such as *Haste makes waste*—*Honesty is the best policy*, with ten thousand more, have nothing figurative about them. Here again the error has arisen from taking that which belongs certainly to very many proverbs, and those oftentimes the best and choicest, and transferring it as a necessary condition, to all. This much of truth they who made the assertion certainly had; namely, that the employment of the concrete instead of the abstract is one of the most frequent means by which it obtains and keeps its popularity; for so the proverb makes its appeal to the whole man—not to the intellectual faculties alone, but to the feelings, to the fancy, or even to the imagination, as well, stirring the whole man to pleasurable activity.

By the help of an instance or two we can best realize to ourselves how great an advantage it thus obtains for itself. Suppose, for example, one were to content himself with saying, "He may wait till he is a beggar, who waits to be rich by other men's deaths;" would this trite morality be likely to go half so far, or to be remembered half so long, as the vigorous comparison of this proverb: "*He who waits for dead men's shoes may go barefoot?*[*] Or again, what were "All men are mortal," as compared with the proverb: *Every door may be shut but death's door?* Or let one observe: "More perish by intemperance than are drowned in the sea," is this anything better than a painful, yet at the same time a flat, truism? But let it be put in this shape: *More are drowned in the wine-cup than in the ocean;*"[†] or again in this: *More are drowned in wine and in beer than in water:*[‡] (and these both are German proverbs) and the assertion assumes quite a different character. There is something that lays hold on us now. We are struck with the smallness of the cup as set against the vastness of the ocean, while yet so many more deaths are ascribed to that than to this; and further with the fact that literally none are, and none could be, drowned in the former, while multitudes perish in the latter. In the justifying of the paradox, in the extricating of the real truth from the apparent falsehood of the statement, in the answer to the appeal made here to the imagination, an appeal and challenge which, unless it be responded to, the proverb must remain unintelligible to us — in all this there is a process of mental activity, oftentimes so rapidly exercised

* The same, under a different image, in Spanish: Larga soga tira, quien por muerte agena suspira.

† Im Becher ersaufen mehr, als im Meere.

‡ In Wein und Bier ertrinken mehr denn im Wasser.

as scarcely to be perceptible, yet not the less carried on with a pleasurable excitement.*

Let me mention now a few other of the more frequent helps which the proverb employs for obtaining currency among men, for being listened to with pleasure by them, for not slipping again from their memories who have once heard it; yet helps which are evidently so separable from it, that none can be in danger of affirming them essential parts or conditions of it. Of these rhyme is the most prominent. It would lead me altogether from my immediate argument, were I to enter into a disquisition on the causes of the charm, which rhyme has for us all; but that it does possess a wondrous charm, that we *like* what is *like*, is attested by a thousand facts, and not least by the circumstance that into this rhyming form a very great multitude of proverbs, and those among the most widely current, have been thrown. Though such will probably at once be present to the minds of all, yet let me mention a few: *Good mind, good find;—Wide will wear, but tight will tear;—Truth may be blamed, but can not be shamed;—Little strokes fell great oaks;—Women's jars breed men's wars;—A king's face should give grace;—East, west, home is best;—*

* Here is the explanation of the perplexity of Erasmus: Deinde fit, *nescio quo pacto*, ut sententia proverbio quasi vibrata feriat acrius auditoris animum, et aculeos quosdam cogitationum relinquat infixos.

Who goes a-borrowing, goes a-sorrowing; with many more, uniting, as you will observe several of them do, this of rhyme with that which I have spoken of before, namely, extreme brevity and conciseness.*

Alliteration, which is nearly allied to rhyme, is another of the helps whereof the proverb largely avails itself Alliteration was at one time an important element in our early English versification; it almost promised to contend with rhyme itself, which should be the most important; and perhaps, if some great master in the art had arisen, might have retained a far greater hold on English poetry than it now possesses. At present it is merely secondary and subsidiary. Yet it can not be called altogether unimportant; no master of melody despises it; on the contrary, the greatest, as in our days Tennyson, make the most frequent, though not always the most obvious use of it. In the proverb you will find it of continual recurrence,

* So, too, in other languages: Qui prend, se rend;—Qui se loue, s'emboue;—chi và piano, và sano;—Chi compra terra, compra guerra;—Quien se muda, Dios le ayuda;—Wie gewonnen, so zerronnen; and the Latin medieval: Qualis vita, finis ita; Via crucis, via lucis. We sometimes think of rhyme as a modern invention, and to the modern world no doubt belongs the discovery of all its capabilities, and the consequent large application of it. But proverbs alone would be sufficient to show that in itself it is not modern, however restricted in old times the employment of it may have been. For instance, there is a Greek proverb to express that men learn by their sufferings more than by any other teaching: Παθήματα, μαθήματα (*Herod.*, i. 207); one which in the Latin, Nocumenta, documenta, finds both in rhyme and sense its equivalent; to which evidently the inducement lay in the chiming and rhyming words.

and where it falls, as, to be worth anything, it must, on the key-words of the sentence, of very high value. Thus: *Frost and fraud both end in foul;* — *Like lips, like lettuce;* — *No cross, no crown;* — *Out of debt, out of danger;* — *Do in hill as you would do in hall;** that is, Be in solitude the same that you would be in a crowd. I will not detain you with further examples of this in other languages; but such occur, and in such numbers that it seems idle to quote them, in all; I will only adduce, in concluding this branch of the subject, a single Italian proverb, which in a remarkable manner unites all three qualities of which we have been last treating, brevity, rhyme, and alliteration: *Traduttori, traditori;* one which we might perhaps reconstitute in English thus: *Translators, traitors;* so untrue, for the most part, are they to the genius of their original, to its spirit, if not to its letter, and frequently to both; so do they *surrender*, rather than *render*, its meaning; not *turning*, but only *overturning* it from one language to another.†

A certain pleasant exaggeration, the use of the figure hyperbole, is a not unfrequent engine with the proverb to procure attention, and to make a way for itself into the minds of men. Thus the Persians have a proverb: *A needle's eye is wide*

* So in Latin: Nil sol et sale utilius.

† This is St. Jerome's pun, who complains that the Latin versions of the Greek Testament current in the church in his day were too many of them not *versiones*, but *eversiones*.

enough for two friends; the whole world is too narrow for two foes; and of a man whose good luck seems never to forsake him, so that from the very things which would be another man's ruin he extricates himself not merely without harm, but with profit and with credit, the Arabs say: *Fling him into the Nile, and he will come up with a fish in his mouth.* We have here examples of hyperbole in the proverb, a figure of natural rhetoric which Scripture itself does not disdain occasionally to employ.

In all this which I have just traced out—in the fact that the proverbs of a language are so frequently its highest bloom and flower, while yet so much of their beauty consists often in curious felicities of diction pertaining exclusively to some single language, either in a rapid conciseness to which nothing tantamount exists elsewhere, or in rhymes which it is hard to reproduce, or in alliterations which do not easily find their equivalents, or in other verbal happiness such as these—lies the difficulty which is often felt, which I shall myself often feel in the course of these lectures, of transferring them without serious loss, nay, sometimes the impossibility of transferring them at all from one language to another.* Oftentimes, to use an

* Thus in respect of this German proverb—

"Stultus und Stolz
Wachset aus Einem Holz"—

its transfer into any other language is manifestly impossible.

image of Erasmus,* they are like those wines (for instance, the Valdepenas of Spain), of which the true excellence can only be known by those who drink them in the land that gave them birth. Transport them under other skies, or still worse, empty them from vessel to vessel, and their strength and flavor will in great part have disappeared in the process.

Still, this is rather the case, where we seek deliberately, and only in a literary interest, to translate some proverb which we admire from its native language into our own or another. Where, on the contrary, it has *transferred itself*, made for itself a second home, and taken root a second time in the heart and affections of a people, in such a case one is continually surprised at the instinctive skill with which it has found compensations for that which it has been compelled to let go; it is impossible not to admire the unconscious skill with which it has replaced one vigorous idiom by another, one happy rhyme or play on words by its equivalent; and all this even in those cases where the extremely narrow limits in which it must confine itself allow it the very smallest liberty of selection. And thus, presenting itself equally finished and complete in

* Habent enim hoc peculiare pleraque proverbia, ut in eâ linguâ sonare postulant in qua nata sunt; quod si in alienum sermonem demigrârint, multum gratiæ decedat. Quemadmodum sunt et vina quædam quæ recusant exportari, nec germanam saporis gratiam obtineant, nisi in his locis in quibus proveniunt.

two or even more languages, the internal evidence will be quite insufficient to determine which of its forms we shall regard as the original, and which as a copy. For example, the proverb at once German and French, which I can present in no comelier English dress than this—

Mother's truth
Keeps constant use;

but which in German runs thus:—

Mutter-treu
Wird täglich neu;

and in French—

Tendresse maternelle
Toujours se renouvelle;

appears to me as exquisitely graceful and tender in the one language as in the other; while yet so much of its beauty depends on the form, that beforehand one could hardly have expected that the charm of it would have survived its transfer to the second language, whichever that may be, wherein it found a home. Having thus opened the subject, I reserve further remarks for the lectures which follow.

LECTURE II.

THE GENERATION OF PROVERBS.

With the form and definition of a proverb, my first lecture was occupied. Let us proceed to consider, in the present, how far it may be possible to realize to ourselves the processes by which a nation gets together the great body of its proverbs, the sources from which it mainly derives them, and the circumstances under which such as it makes for itself of new had their birth and generation.

And first, I would call to your attention the fact that a vast number of its proverbs a people does not make for itself, but finds ready made to its hands; it enters upon them as a part of its intellectual and moral inheritance. The world has now lasted so long, and the generations of men have thought, felt, enjoyed, suffered, and altogether learned so much, that there is an immense stock of wisdom which may be said to belong to humanity in common, being the fruits of all this its experience in the past. Even Aristotle, more than two thousand years ago, could speak of proverbs as the fragments of an elder wisdom, which on account of their brevity and aptness, had amid a general wreck and ruin been preserved. These, the common property of the civilized world, are the original stock with which each nation starts; these, either orally handed down to it, or made its own by those of its earlier writers who set it in living communication with the past. Thus, and through these channels, a vast number of Greek, Latin, and medieval proverbs live on with us, and with all the modern nations of the world.

It is, indeed, oftentimes a veritable surprise to discover the venerable age and antiquity of a proverb, which we have hitherto assumed to be quite a later birth of modern society. Thus we may perhaps suppose that well-known word which forbids the too accurate scanning of a present, *One must not look a gift-horse in the mouth*, to be of English extraction the genuine growth of our own soil. I will not pretend to say how old it may be, but it is certainly as old as Jerome, a Latin father of the fourth century; who, when some found fault with certain writings of his, replied with a tartness which he could occasionally exhibit, that they were voluntarily on his part, free-will offerings, and with this quoted the proverb, that it did not behoove to look a gift-horse in the mouth; and before it comes to us, we meet it once more in one of the rhymed Latin verses, which were such great favorites in the middle ages:—

"Si quis dat mannos, ne quære in dentibus annos."

Again, *Liars should have good memories* is a proverb which probably we assume to be modern; yet it is very far from so being. The same Jerome, who, I may observe by the way, is a very great quoter of proverbs, and who has preserved some that would not otherwise have descended to us,* speaks of one as unmindful of the old proverbs, *Liars should have good memories*,† and we find it ourselves in a writer a good deal older than him.‡

Having lighted on one of those Latin rhymed verses, let me, by the way, guard against an error about them, into which it would be very easy to fall. I have seen it suggested that these, if not the source from which, are yet the channels by which, a great many proverbs have reached us. I should greatly doubt it. This much we may conclude

* Thus is it, I believe, with "Bos lassus fortius figit pedem;" a proverb with which he warns the younger Augustine not to provoke a contest with him, the weary, but therefore the more formidable, antagonist.

† Oblitus veteris proverbii: mendaces memores esse oportere. Let me quote here Fuller's excellent unfolding of this proverb: "Memory in a liar is no more than needs. For first lies are hard to be remembered, because many, whereas truth is but one; secondly, because a lie cursorily told takes little footing and settled fastness in the teller's memory, but prints itself deeper in the hearers, who take the greater notice because of the improbability and deformity thereof; and one will remember the sight of a monster longer than the sight of a handsome body. Hence comes it to pass that when the liar hath forgotten himself, his auditors put him in mind of the lie and take him therein."

‡ Quintilian, *Inst.* 1. 4.

from the existence of proverbs in this shape, namely, that since these rhymed or leonine verses went altogether out of fashion at the revival of a classical taste in the fifteenth century, such proverbs as are found in this form may be affirmed with a tolerable certainty to date at least as far back as that period; but not that in all, or even in a majority of cases, this shape was their earliest. Oftentime the proverb in its more popular form is so greatly superior to the same in this its Latin monkish dress, that the latter, by its tameness and flatness, betrays itself at once as the inadequate translation, and we can not fail to regard the other as the genuine proverb. Many of them are "so essentially Teutonic, that they frequently appear to great disadvantage in the Latin garb which has been huddled upon them."* Thus, when we have on one side the English, *Hungry bellies have no ears*, and on the other the Latin—

"Jejunus venter non audit verba libenter,"

who can doubt that the first is the proverb, and the second only its versification? or who would hesitate to affirm that the old Greek proverb, *A rolling stone gathers no moss*, may very well have come to us without the intermediation of the medieval Latin—

"Non fit hirsutus lapis hinc atque inde volutus?"

And the true state of the case comes out still more

* Kemble, *Solomon and Saturn*, p. 56.

clearly, where there are *two* of these rhymed Latin equivalents for the one popular proverb, and these quite independent of each other. So it is in respect of our English proverb, *A bird in the hand is worth two in the bush*, which appears in this form:—

"Una avis in dextrâ melior quam quatuor extra:"

and also in this:—

"Capta avis est pluris quam mille in gramine ruris."

Who can fail to see here two independent attempts to render the same saying? Sometimes the Latin line confesses itself to be only the rendering of a popular word; thus is it with the following:—

"*Ut dicunt multi*, cito transit lancea stulti:"

in other words: *A fool's bolt is soon shot.*

Then, besides this derivation from elder sources, from the literature of nations which as such now no longer exist, besides this process in which a people are merely receivers and borrowers, there is also, at somewhat later periods in its life, a mutual interchange between it and other nations growing up beside, and contemporaneously with it, of their own several inventions in this kind; a free giving and taking, in which it is often hard, and oftener impossible, to say which is lender and which borrower. Thus the quantity of proverbs not drawn from antiquity, but common to all, or nearly all, of the modern European languages, is very great. The "solidarity" (to use a word which it is in vain to strive against) of all the nations of Christendom comes out very noticeably here.

There is indeed nothing in the study of proverbs, in the attribution of them to their right owners, in the arrangement and citation of them, which creates a greater perplexity than the circumstances of finding the same proverb in so many different quarters, current among so many different nations. In quoting it as of one, it often seems as if we were doing wrong to many, while yet it is almost, or oftener still altogether, impossible to determine to what nation it first belonged, so that others drew it at second hand from that one; even granting that any form in which we now possess it is really its oldest of all. More than once this fact has occasioned a serious disappointment to the zealous collector of the proverbs of his native country. Proud of the rich treasures which in this kind it possessed, he has very reluctantly discovered, on a fuller investigation of the whole subject, how many of these which he counted native, the peculiar heirloom and glory of his own land, must at once and without hesitation be resigned to others, who can be shown beyond all doubt to have been in earlier possession of them: while in respect of many more, if his own nation can put in a claim to them as well as others, yet he is compelled to feel that it can put in no better than, oftentimes not so good as, many competitors.*

This single fact, which it is impossible to question, that nations are thus continually borrowing proverbs from one another, is sufficient to show, that, however the great body of those which are the portion of a nation may be, some almost as old as itself, and some far older, it would for all this be a serious mistake to regard the sum of them as a closed account, neither capable of, nor actually receiving, addition—a mistake of the same character as that sometimes made in regard to the *words* of a language. So long as language is living, it will be appropriating foreign words, putting forth new words of its own. Exactly in the same way, so long as a people have any vigorous energies at work in the midst of them, are acquiring any new experiences of life, are forming any new moral convictions; for the new experiences and convictions new utterances will be found, some of the happiest of which will receive that stamp of general allowance which shall constitute them proverbs. And this fact makes it little likely that the collections which exist in print, and certainly not the earlier ones, will embrace all the proverbs in actual circulation. They preserve, indeed, many others—all

* Kelly, in the preface to his very useful collection of Scotch proverbs, describes his own disappointment at making exactly such a discovery as this.

those which, having now become obsolete, would, but for them, have been forgotten. But there are not a few, as I imagine, which, living on the lips of men, have yet never found their way into books, however worthy to have done so; either because the sphere in which they circulate has continued always a narrow one, or that the occasions which call them out are very rare, or that they, having only lately risen up, have not hitherto attracted the attention of any who cared to record them. It would be well, if such as take an interest in the subject, and are sufficiently well versed in the proverbial literature of their own country, to recognise such unregistered proverbs when they meet them, would secure them from that perishing, which, so long as they remain merely oral, might easily overtake them; and would make them, at the same time, what all *good* proverbs ought certainly to be, the common heritage of all.*

* The pages of the excellent *Notes and Queries* would no doubt be open to receive such, and in them they might be safely garnered up. That there are such proverbs to reward him who should carefully watch for them, is abundantly proved by the immense addition, which, as I shall have occasion hereafter to mention, a Spanish scholar was able to make to the collected proverbs, so numerous before, of Spain. Nor do there want other indications of the like kind. Thus, the editor of very far the best modern collection of German proverbs, records this one, which is found, as he affirms, in no preceding collection, and which he himself never heard but once, and then from the lips of an aged lay servitor of a monastery in the Black Forest: *Offend one monk, and the lappets of all cowls will flutter as far as Rome* (Beleidigestu einen Münch, so knappen alle

And as new proverbs will be born from life and from life's experience, so too there will be another fruitful source of their further increase, namely, the books which the people have made heartily their own. Portions of these they will continually detach, most often word for word; at other times wrought up into new shapes with that freedom which they claim to exercise in regard of whatever they thus appropriate to their own use. These, having detached, they will give and take as part of their current intellectual money. Thus, "*Evil communications corrupt good manners*" is, word for word, from a Greek comedy. It is not probable that St. Paul had ever read this comedy; but the words, for their truth's sake, had been taken up into the common speech of men; and not as a citation, but as a proverb, he uses them. And if you will, from this point of view, glance over a few pages of one of Shakespeare's more popular dramas—Hamlet, for example—you will be surprised, in case

Kuttenzipfel bis nach Rom); and yet who can doubt that we have a genuine proverb here, and one excellently expressive of the common cause which the whole of the monastic orders, despite their inner dissensions, made ever, when assailed from without, with one another? It is very easy to be deceived in such a matter, and one must be content often to be so; but the following, which is current in Ireland, I have never seen in print: "*The man on the dyke always hurls well;*" the looker-on at a game of hurling, seated indolently on the wall, always imagines that he could improve on the strokes of the actual players, and, if you will listen to him, would have played the game much better than they; a proverb of sufficiently wide application.

your attention has never been called to this before, to note how much has in this manner been separated from it, that it might pass into the every-day use and service of man; and you will be prepared to estimate higher than ever what he has done for his fellow-countrymen, the "possession for ever" which his writings have become for them. And much, no doubt, is passing even now from favorite authors into the flesh and blood of a nation's moral and intellectual life; and as "household words," as parts of its proverbial philosophy, for ever incorporating itself therewith. We have a fair measure of an author's true popularity—I mean, of the real and lasting hold which he has taken on his nation's heart, in the extent to which it has been thus done with his writings.

There is another way in which additions are from time to time made to the proverbial wealth of a people. Some event has laid strong hold of their imagination, has stirred up the depths of their moral consciousness; and this they have gathered up for themselves, perhaps in some striking phrase which was uttered at the moment, or in some allusive words, understood by everybody, and which at once summon up the whole incident before their eyes.

Sacred history furnishes us with one example at the least of the generation in this wise of a proverb. That word, "Is Saul also among the prophets?" is one of which we know the exact manner in which it grew to be "a proverb in Israel." When the son of Kish revealed of a sudden that nobler life which had hitherto been slumbering in him, alike undreamed of by himself and by others, took his part and place among the sons of the prophets, and, borne along in their enthusiasm, praised and prophesied as they did, showing that he was indeed turned into another man, then all that knew him beforehand, said one to another, some probably in sincere astonishment, some in irony and unbelief, "Is Saul also among the prophets?" And the question they asked found and finds its application so often as any reveals of a sudden, at some crisis of his life, qualities for which those who knew him the longest had hitherto given him no credit, a nobleness which had been latent in him until now, a power of taking his place among the worthiest and the best, which none until now had at all deemed him to possess. It will, of course, find equally its application, when one does not step truly, but only affects to step suddenly into a higher school, to take his place in a nobler circle of life than that in which hitherto he has moved.

Another proverb, and one well known to the Greek scholar, *The cranes of Ibycus,** had its rise in one of those remarkable incidents, which, witnessing for God's inscrutable judgments, are eagerly

* Αἱ Ἰβύκου γέρανοι.

grasped by men. The story of its birth is indeed one to which so deep a moral interest is attached, that I shall not hesitate to repeat it, even at the risk that Schiller's immortal poem on the subject, or it may be the classical studies of some here, may have made it already familiar to a portion of my hearers. Ibycus, a famous lyrical poet of Greece, journeying to Corinth, was assailed by robbers: as he fell beneath their murderous strokes he looked round if any witnesses or avengers were nigh. No living thing was in sight, but a flight of cranes soaring high over head. He called on them, and to them committed the avenging of his blood. A vain commission, as it might have appeared, and as no doubt it did to the murderers appear. Yet it was not so; for these, sitting a little time after in the open theatre at Corinth, beheld this flight of cranes hovering above them, and one said scoffingly to another, "Lo, there, the avengers of Ibycus!" The words were caught up by some near them; for already the poet's disappearance had awakened anxiety and alarm. Being questioned, they betrayed themselves, and were led to their doom; and *The cranes of Ibycus* passed into a proverb, very much as our *Murder will out*, to express the wondrous leadings of God whereby the secretest thing of blood is continually brought to the light.

Memorable words of illustrious men will frequently not die in the utterance, but pass from mouth to mouth, being still repeated with complacency, till at length they have received their adoption into the great family of national proverbs. Such were the gnomes or sayings of the Seven Wise Men of Greece, supposing them to have been indeed theirs, and not ascribed to them only after they had obtained universal currency and acceptance. So too a saying, attributed to Alexander the Great, may very well have arisen on the occasion, and under the circumstances, to which its birth is commonly ascribed. When some of his officers reported to him with something of dismay the innumerable multitude of the Persian hosts which were advancing to assail him, the youthful Macedonian hero silenced them and their apprehensions with the reply: *One butcher does not fear many sheep;* not in this applying an old proverb, but framing a new, and one admirably expressive of the confidence which he felt in the immeasurable superiority of the Hellenic over the barbarian man; and this word, having been once set on foot by him, has since lived on, and that because the occasions were so numerous on which a word like this would find its application.

And, taking occasion from this royal proverb, let me just observe, by the way, that it would be a great mistake to assume, though the error is by no means an uncommon one, that because proverbs are popular, they have therefore originally sprung from the bosom of the populace. What was urged in my first lecture of their popularity was not at all intended in this sense; and the sound, common sense, the wit, the wisdom, the right feeling, which are their *predominant* characteristics, alike contradict any such supposition. They spring rather from the sound, healthy kernel of the nation, whether in high place or in low; and it is surely worthy of note, how large a proportion of those with the generation of which we are acquainted, owe their existence to the foremost men of their time, to its philosophers, its princes, and its kings; as it would not be difficult to show. And indeed the evil in proverbs testifies to this quite as much as the good. Thus, the many proverbs, in almost all modern tongues, expressing scorn of the "villain," are alone sufficient to show that, for the most part, they are very far from having their birth quite in the lower regions of society, but reflect much oftener the prejudices and passions of those higher in the social scale.

Let me adduce another example of the proverbs which have thus grown out of an incident, which contain an allusion to it, and are only perfectly intelligible when the incident itself is known. It is this Spanish: *Let that which is lost be for God:* one the story of whose birth is thus given by the leading Spanish commentator on the proverbs of his nation: The father of a family, making his will and disposing of his goods upon his death-bed, ordained concerning a certain cow which had strayed, and had been now for a long time missing, that, if it were found, it should be for his children: if otherwise, for God: and hence the proverb, *Let that which is lost be for God*, arose. The saying was not one to let die: it laid bare with too fine a skill some of the subtlest treacheries of the human heart; for, indeed, whenever men would give to God only their lame and their blind, that which costs them nothing, that from which they hope no good, no profit, no pleasure for themselves, what are they saying in their hearts but that which this man said openly—*Let that which is lost be for God.*

The subject of the generation of proverbs, upon which I have thus touched so slightly, is yet one upon which whole volumes have been written. Those who have occupied themselves herein have sought to trace historically the circumstances out of which various proverbs have sprung, and to which they owe their existence; that so by the analogy of these we might realize to ourselves the rise of others whose origins lie out of our vision, obscure and unknown. No one will deny the interest of the subject: it can not but be most interesting to preside thus at the birth of a saying which has lived on and held its ground in the world, and has not ceased, from the day it was first uttered, to be more or less of a spiritual or intellectual force among men. Still the cases where this is possible are exceedingly rare, as compared with the far greater number where the first birth is veiled, as is almost all birth, in mystery and obscurity. And indeed it could scarcely be otherwise. The great majority of proverbs are foundlings, the happier foundlings of a nation's wit, which the collective nation has refused to let perish, has taken up and adopted for its own. But still, as must be expected to be the case with foundlings, they can, for the most part, give no account of themselves. They rest on their own merits, not on those of their parents and authors, whom they have forgotten, and who seem equally to have forgotten them; or, at least, fail to claim them. Not seldom, too, when a story has been given to account for a proverb's rise, it must remain a question, open to much doubt whether the story has not been subsequently imagined for the proverb, rather than that the proverb has indeed sprung out of history.*

The proverb having thus had its rise from life, however it may be often impossible to trace that rise, will continually turn back to life again; it will attest its own practical character by the frequency with which it will present itself for use, and will

* Livy's account of Cantherium in fossâ, and of the manner in which it became a rustic proverb in Italy (l. 23. c. 47), is a case in point, where it is very hard to give credit to the parentage which has been assigned to the saying. See *Döderlein's Lat. Synonyme*, v. 4, p. 289.

have been actually used upon earnest and important occasions, throwing its weight into one scale or the other at some critical moment, and sometimes with decisive effect. I have little doubt that, with knowledge sufficient, one might bring together a large collection of instances wherein, at significant moments, the proverb has played its part, and, it may be, very often helped to bring about issues, of which all would acknowledge the importance.

In this aspect, as having been used at a great critical moment, and as part of the moral influence brought to bear on that occasion for effecting a great result, no proverb of man's can be compared with that one which the Lord used when he met his future apostle, but at this time his persecutor, in the way, and warned him of the fruitlessness and folly of a longer resistance to a might which must overcome him, and with still greater harm to himself, at the last: *It is hard for thee to kick against the pricks.** (Acts xxvi. 14.) It is not always observed, but yet it adds much to the fitness of this proverb's use on this great occasion, that it was already, even in that heathen world to which originally it belonged, predominantly used to note the madness of a striving on man's part against the superior power of the gods; for so we find it in the chief passages of heathen antiquity in which it occurs.†

* *Σκληρόν σοι πρὸς κέντρα γακτίζειν.*

† Æschylus, *Prom. V.* 322; Euripides, *Bacch.* 795; Pindar, *Pyth.* 2, 94–96. The image is, of course that of the stubborn ox, which,

I must take the second illustration of my assertion from a very different quarter, passing at a single stride from the kingdom of heaven to the kingdom of hell, and finding my example there. We are told, then, that when Catherine de Medicis desired to overcome the hesitation of her son Charles the Ninth, and draw from him his consent to the massacre, afterward known as that of St. Bartholomew, she urged on him with effect a proverb which she had brought with her from her own land, and assuredly one of the most convenient maxims for tyrants that was ever framed: *Clemency is sometimes cruelty, and cruelty clemency.*

Later French history supplies another and more agreeable illustration. At the siege of Douay, Louis the Fourteenth found himself with his suite unexpectedly under a heavy cannonade from the besieged city. I do not believe that Louis was deficient in personal courage, yet, in compliance with the entreaties of most of those around him, who urged that he should not expose so important a life, he was about, in somewhat unsoldierly and unkingly fashion, immediately to retire; when M. de Charost, drawing close to him, whispered the well-known French proverb in his ear: *The wine is drawn; it must be drunk.*‡ The king remained

when urged to go forward, recalcitrates against the sharp-pointed iron goad, and, already wounded, thus only wounds itself the more.

* Le vin est versé; il faut le boire.

exposed to the fire of the enemy a suitable period, and it is said ever after held in higher honor than before the counsellor who had with this word saved him from an unseemly retreat. Let this on the generation of proverbs, with the actual employment which has been made of them, for the present suffice.

LECTURE III.

THE PROVERBS OF DIFFERENT NATIONS COMPARED.

"The genius, wit, and spirit of a nation are discovered in its proverbs," this is Lord Bacon's well-worn remark; although, indeed, only well-worn because of its truth. "In them," it has been further said, "is to be found an inexhaustible source of precious documents in regard of the interior history, the manners, the opinions, the beliefs,* the customs of the people among whom they have had their course." Let us put these assertions to the proof, and see how far in this people's or in that

* The writer might have added, the superstitions; for proverbs not a few involve and rest on popular superstitions, and a collection of these would be curious and in many ways instructive. Such, for instance, is the Latin (it is, indeed, also Greek): *A serpent, unless it devour a serpent, grows not to a dragon* (Serpens, nisi serpentem comederit, non fit draco); which Lord Bacon moralizes so shrewdly; "The folly of one man is the fortune of another; for no man prospers so suddenly as by other men's errors." Such again is the old German proverb: *The night is no man's friend* (Die Nacht ist keines Menschen Freund); which rests, as Grimm has so truly observed (*Deutsche Mythol.*, p. 713), on the wide-spread feeling in the northern mythologies, of the night as an unfriendly and, indeed, hostile power to man. And such, too, the French: *A Sunday's child dies never of the plague* (Qui nait le dimanche, jamais ne meurt de peste).

people's proverbs, its innermost heart speaks out to us; how far the comparison of the proverbs of one nation with those of others may be made instructive to us; what this comparison will tell us severally about each. This only I will ask, ere we enter upon the subject, that if I should fail here in drawing out anything strongly characteristic, if the proverbs regarded from this point of view should not seem to reveal to you any of the true secrets of national life, you will not therefore misdoubt those assertions with which my lecture opened; or assume that these documents would not yield up their secret, if questioned aright; but only believe that the test has been unskilfully applied; or, if you will, that my brief limits have not allowed me to make clear that which with larger space I might not have wholly failed in doing.

I am very well aware that in following upon this track, one is ever liable to deceive oneself, to impose upon others, picking out and adducing such proverbs as conform to a preconceived theory, passing over those which would militate against it. Quite allowing that there is such a danger which needs to be guarded against, and also that there are a multitude of these sayings which can not be made to illustrate difference, for they rest on the broad foundation of the universal humanity, underlying and deeper than that which is peculiar and national, I am yet persuaded that enough remain, and such as may with perfect good faith be adduced, to confirm these assertions; that we *may* learn from the proverbs current among a people what is nearest and dearest to their hearts, the aspects under which they contemplate life, how honor and dishonor are distributed among them, what is of good, what of evil report in their eyes, with very much more which it can never be unprofitable to know.

To begin, then, with the proverbs of Greece. That which strikes one most in the study of these, and which the more they are studied, the more fills the thoughtful student with wonder, is the evidence they yield of a leavening through and through of the entire nation with the most intimate knowledge of its own mythology, history, and poetry. The infinite multitude of slight and fine allusions to the legends of their gods and heroes, to the earlier incidents of their own history, to the Homeric narrative, the delicate side glances at all these which the Greek proverbs constantly embody,* assume an acquaintance, indeed a familiarity, with all this on their parts among whom they passed current, which almost exceeds belief. In many and most important respects, the Greek proverbs considered as a whole are inferior to those of many nations of modern Christendom. This is nothing wonderful; Christianity would have done little for the world,

* Thus 'Αΐδος κυνῆ.—Ἄπληστος πίθος.—'Ιλιὰς κακῶν.

would have proved very ineffectual for the elevating, purifying, and deepening of man's life, if it had been otherwise. But, with all this, as bearing testimony to the high intellectual training of the people who employed them, to a culture not restricted to certain classes, but which must have been diffused through the whole nation, no other collection can bear the remotest comparison with this.

It is altogether different with the Roman proverbs. These, the genuine Roman, the growth of their own soil, are very far fewer in number than the Greek, as was indeed to be expected from the far less subtle and less fertile genius of the people. Hardly any of them are legendary or mythological; which again agrees with the fact that the Italian pantheon was very scantily peopled as compared with the Greek. Very few have much poetry about them, or any very rare delicacy or refinement of feeling. In respect of love indeed, not the Roman only, but Greek and Roman alike, are immeasurably inferior to those which many modern nations could supply. Thus a proverb of such religious depth and beauty as our own, *Marriages are made in heaven*, it would have been quite impossible for all antiquity to have produced, or even remotely to have approached. In the setting out not of love, but of friendship, and of the claims which it makes, the blessings which it brings, is exhibited whatever depth and tenderness they may have.* This indeed, as has been truly observed,† was only to be expected, seeing how much higher an ideal of that existed than of this, the full realization of which was reserved for the modern Christian world. Yet the Roman proverbs are not without other substantial merits of their own. A vigorous moral sense speaks out in many;‡ and even when this is not so prominent, they wear often a thoroughly old Roman aspect; being business-like and practical, frugal and severe, wise saws such as the elder Cato must have loved, such as must have been often upon his lips;§ while in the number that relate to farming they bear singular witness to that strong and lively interest in agricultural pursuits, which was so remarkable a feature in the old Italian life.‖

* In this respect the Latin proverb, Mores amici noveris, non oderis, on which Horace has furnished so exquisite a comment (*Sat*, i. 3, 24–93), and which finds its graceful equivalent in the Italian. Ama l'amico tuo con il difetto suo, is worthy of all admiration.

† By Zell, in his slight but graceful little treatise, *On the proverbs of the ancient Romans*, *Ferienschriften*, v. 2, p. 1–96.

‡ Thus, Noxa caput sequitur; — Conscientia, mille testes.

§ He has preserved for us that very sensible, and at the same time truly characteristic one, Quod non opus est, asse carum est.

‖ These are two or three of the most notable — the first against "high farming," which it is strange if it has not been appealed to in the modern controversy on the subject: Nihil minus expedit quam agrum optime colere. (Pliny, *H. N.*, 6. 18.) Over against this, however, we must set another, warning against the attempt to farm with insufficient capital; Oportet agrum imbecilliorem esse quam agricolam; and yet another, on the liberal answer which the land will make to the pains and cost bestowed on it; Qui arat olivetum, rogat fructum; qui stercorat, exorat; qui cædit, cogit.

It will not be possible to pass under even this hastiest review more than two or three of the modern families of proverbs. Let us turn first to the proverbs of Spain. I instance these, because the Spanish literature, poor in many provinces wherein many others are rich, is probably richer in this province than any other literature in the world, certainly than any other in the western world; and this, I should be inclined to believe, both as respects quantity and quality.* In respect of quantity, the mere number of Spanish proverbs is astonishing. A collection I have been using while preparing these lectures, contains between seven and eight thousand, and yet does not contain all; for I have searched it in vain for several with which from other sources I had become acquainted. Nay, it must be very far indeed from exhausting the entire stock, seeing that there exists a manuscript collection brought tegether by a distinguished Spanish scholar, in which the proverbs have attained to the almost incredible amount of from five and twenty to thirty thousand.†

* This was the judgment of Salmasius, who says: Inter Europæos Hispani, in his excellent, Itali vix cedunt, Galli proximo sequuntur intervallo.

† What may have become of this collection I know not; but it was formerly in Richard Heber's library (see the *Catalogue*, v. 9. No. 1697). Juan Yriarte was the collector, and in a note to the *Catalogue* it is stated that he devoted himself with such eagerness to the bringing of it to the highest possible state of completeness, that he would give his servants a fee for any new proverb they brought

And in respect of their quality, it needs only to call to mind some of those, so rich in humor, so double-shotted with sense, wherewith the squire in *Don Quixote* adorns his discourse; being oftentimes indeed not the fringe and border, but the main woof and texture of it: and then, if we assume that the remainder are not altogether unlike these, we shall, I think, feel that it would be difficult to rate them more highly than they deserve. And some are in a loftier vein; for taking, as we have a right to do, Cervantes himself as the truest exponent of the Spanish character, we should be prepared to trace in the proverbs of Spain a grave thoughtfulness, a stately humor, to find them breathing the very spirit of chivalry and honor, and indeed of freedom too; for in Spain, as throughout so much of Europe, it is despotism, and not freedom, which is new. Nor are we disappointed in these our expectations. How eminently chivalresque, for instance, the following: *White hands can not hurt.** What a grave humor lurks in this: *The ass knows in whose face he brays.*† What a stately apathy—how proud a manner of looking calamity in the face—speaks out in the admonition which this

him; while to each, as it was inserted in his list, he was careful to attach a memorandum of the quarter from which it came; and if this was not from books but from life, an indication of the name, the rank, the condition in life of the person from whom it was derived.

* Las manos blancas no ofenden.

† Bien sabe el asno en cuya cara rebozna.

one contains: *If thou seest thine house in flames, approach and warm thyself by it.** What a spirit of freedom, which refuses to be encroached on even by the highest, is embodied in another: *The king goes as far as he may, not as far as he would.*†

We may, too, I think, remark how a nation will occasionally, in its proverbs, indulge in a fine irony upon itself, and show that it is perfectly aware of its own weaknesses, follies, and faults. This the Spaniards must be allowed to do in their proverb, *Succors of Spain, or late or never.*‡ However largely and confidently promised, these *succors of Spain* either do not arrive at all, or only arrive after the opportunity in which they could have served have passed away. Certainly any one who reads the despatches of England's Great Captain during the peninsular war, will find in almost every page of them that which abundantly justifies this proverb—will own that those who made it read themselves aright, and could not have designated broken pledges, unfulfilled promises of aid, tardy and thus ineffectual assistance, by a happier title than *Succors of Spain.* And then again, what a fearful glimpse of those blood-feuds, which, having once begun, seems as if they could never end, blood touching blood, and violence evermore provoking

* Quando vierás tu casa quemar, llega te á escalentar.

† El rey va hasta do puede, y no hasta do quiere.

‡ Socorros de España, ó tarde, ó nunca.

its like, have we in the following: *Kill, and thou shalt be killed, and they shall kill him who kills thee.**

The Italians also are eminently rich in proverbs; and yet, if ever I have been tempted to retract or seriously to modify what I shall have occasion by-and-by to affirm in regard of a nobler life and spirit as predominating in proverbs, it has been after the study of some Italian collection. "The Italian proverbs," it has been said, not without too much reason, though perhaps also with overmuch severity, "have taken a tinge from their deep and politic genius, and their wisdom seems wholly concentrated in their personal interests. I think every tenth proverb in an Italian collection is some cynical or some selfish maxim, a book of the world for worldlings."† Certainly many of them are shrewd enough, and only too shrewd; inculcating a universal suspicion, teaching to look everywhere for a foe—to expect, as the Greeks said, a scorpion under every stone—glorifying artifice and cunning as the true guides and only safe leaders through the perplexed labyrinth of life,‡ and altogether seem-

* Matarás, y matarte han, y matarán a quien te matare.

† *Curiosities of Literature,* p. 391. London: 1838.

‡ These may serve as examples: "Chi ha sospetto, di rado è in difetto."—"Fidarsi è bene, ma non fidarsi è meglio."—"Da chi mi fido, mi guardi Iddio; da chi non mi fido, mi guarderò io."—"Con arte e con inganno si vive mezzo l'anno; con inganno e con arte si vive l'altra parte."

ing dictated as by the very spirit of Machiavel himself.

And worse than this is the glorification of revenge which speaks out in too many of them. I know nothing of its kind calculated to give one a more shuddering sense of horror than the series which might be drawn together of Italian proverbs on this matter, especially when we take them with the commentary which Italian history supplies, and which shows them no empty words, but the deepest utterances of the nation's heart. There is no misgivings in these about the right of entertaining so deadly a guest in the bosom; on the contrary, one of them, exalting the sweetness of revenge, declares, *Revenge is a morsel for God.** There is nothing in them (it would be far better if there were) of blind and headlong passion, but rather a spirit of deliberate calculation, which makes the blood run cold. Thus one gives this advice: *Wait time and place to act thy revenge, for it is never well done in a hurry;* † while another proclaims an immortality of hatred, which no spaces of intervening time shall have availed to weaken: *Revenge of a hundred years old hath still its sucking-teeth.*‡ We may well be thankful that we have in England,

* Vendetta, boccon di Dio.

† Aspetta tempo e loco à far tua vendetta, che la non si fa mai ben in fretta. Compare another: Vuoi far vendetta del tuo nemico, governati bene ed è bell' e fatta.

‡ Vendetta di cent' anni ha ancor i lattaiuoli.

at least as far as I am aware, no sentiments parallel to these, embodied as the permanent convictions of the national mind.

How curious again is the confession which speaks out in another Italian proverb, that the maintenance of the Romish system and the study of Holy Scripture can not go together. It is this: *With the gospel, one becomes a heretic.*‡ No doubt, with the study of the Word of God, one does become a heretic, in the Italian sense of the word; and therefore it is only done to put all obstacles in the way of that study, to assign three years' and four years' imprisonment, with hard labor, to such as shall dare to peruse it; yet certainly it is not a little remarkable that such a confession should have embodied itself in the popular utterances of the nation.

But, while it must be freely owned that the charges brought just now against the Italian proverbs are sufficiently borne out by too many, they are not at all to be included in the common shame. Very many there are not merely of a delicate refinement of beauty, as this, expressive of the freedom in regard of *thine* and *mine* which will exist between true friends: *Friends tie their purses with a spider's thread,*† of a subtle wisdom which has *not* degenerated into cunning and deceit, but also of

* Con l'evangelo si diventa eretico.

† Gli amici legono la borsa con un filo di ragnatelo.

a nobler stamp. Honor and honesty, plain-dealing and uprightness, have here their praises too, and are not seldom pronounced to be in the end more than a match for all cunning and deceit. How excellent in this sense is the following: *For an honest man, half his wits is enough, the whole is too little for a knave:** the ways, that is, of truth and uprightness are so simple and plain, that a little wit is abundantly sufficient for those that walk in them; the ways of falsehood and fraud are so perplexed and tangled, that, sooner or later, all the wit of the cleverest rogue will not preserve him from being entangled therein. How often and how wonderfully has this found its confirmation in the lives of evil men! so true it is, to employ another proverb, and a very deep one, from the same quarter, that *The devil is subtle, but weaves a coarse web.*†

Again, what description of Egypt as it now is, or indeed generally of the East, could set us at the heart of its moral condition—could make us to understand all which long centuries of oppression and misrule have made of it and of its people?—what could do this so effectually as the collection of Arabic proverbs now current in Egypt, which the

* Ad un uomo dabbene avanza la metà del cer cervello; ad un tristo non basta ne anche tutto.

† Jeremy Taylor appears to have found much delight in the proverbs of Italy. In the brief foot-notes which he has appended to the *Holy Living* alone, I counted five and twenty such, to which he makes more or less remote allusion in the text.

traveller Burckhardt gathered, and which, after his death, were published with his name?* In other books, others describe the modern Egyptians, but here they unconsciously describe themselves. The selfishness, the utter extinction of all public spirit, the servility, which no longer, as with an inward shame, creeps into men's acts, but utters itself boldly as the avowed law of their lives, the sense of the oppression of the strong, of the insecurity of the weak, and generally the whole character of life, alike the outward and inward, as poor, mean, sordid, and ignoble, with only a few faintest glimpses of that romance which one usually attaches to the East; all this, as we study these documents, rises up before us in truest though in painfullest outline.

Where, but in a land which evermore was changing its rulers, and in which oftentimes the unworthiest sat in highest places of all, whom yet to propitiate was the only safety, where else could the law of baseness have proclaimed itself aloud, and this have been laid down as the maxim of conduct, *If the monkey reigns, dance before him.* The monkey, it is true, may reign in other lands besides those of the East; but the examples in a neighboring land, not merely of statesmen and warriors, of men such as Guizot and Changarnier, but of many more in every class, erect amid a too general prostration, abundantly testify, that, reign as

† *Arabic Proverbs of the Modern Egyptians.* London: 1830.

the monkey may—Simia in purpurâ,—*all* will not therefore count it their part and their wisdom to dance before him. What indeed this dancing is worth, another of those Eastern adages reveals, which says, *Kiss the hand which thou canst not bite.* Again, in no land save in one, where rulers, being evil in themselves, feel all goodness to be their instinctive foe, and themselves, therefore, entertain an instinctive hostility to it—where they punish, but never reward—where not to be noticed by them is the highest ambition of those under their yoke, in no other land could a proverb like the following, *Do no good, and thou shalt find no evil*, have ever come to the birth. How settled a conviction that wrong, and not right, was the lord paramount of the world, must have grown up in men's spirits, before such a word as this (I know of no sadder one) could have found utterance from their lips.*

I have taken a wide circuit of nations; with the proverb of a people nearer home I must bring this branch of the subject to an end. It is one, and a very characteristic one, which the poet Spenser, who long dwelt in Ireland, records as current in his time among the Irish; in which were contained their offer of service to their native chiefs, with a

* Yet this very mournful collection of Burckhardt's possesses at least one very beautiful proverb on the all-conquering power of love: *Man is the slave of beneficence.*

statement of what they expected in return: *Spend me, and defend me.* Their leaders in all times have taken them only too well at their word in respect of the first half of the proverb, and have not failed prodigally to *spend* them; although their undertakings to *defend* have issued exactly as must ever issue all promises on the part of others to defend men from those evils, from which none can really protect them but themselves.

Other families of proverbs would each of them tell its own tale, give up its own secret; but I must not seek from this point of view to question them further. I would rather bring now to your notice that even where they do not spring, as they can not all, from the centre of a people's heart, nor declare to us the secretest things which are there, but dwell more on the surface of things, in this case also they have often local or national features, which to study and trace out may prove both curious and instructive. Of how many, for example, we may note the manner in which they clothe themselves in an outward form and shape, borrowed from, or suggested by, the peculiar scenery or circumstances or history of their own land; so that they could scarcely have come into existence, not certainly in the shape which they now wear, anywhere besides. Thus our own, *Make hay while the sun shines*, is truly English, and could have had its birth only under such variable skies as ours—not, at any rate, in those southern lands where, during the summer time at least, the sun always shines. In the same way there is a fine Cornish proverb in regard of obstinate wrongheads, who will take no counsel except from calamities, who dash themselves to pieces against obstacles, which, with a little prudence and foresight, they might easily have avoided. It is this: *He who will not be ruled by the rudder must be ruled by the rock.* It sets us at once upon some rocky and wreck-strewn coast; we feel that it could never have been the proverb of an inland people. And this, *Do not talk Arabic in the house of a Moor:** that is, because there thy imperfect knowledge will be detected at once: this we should confidently affirm to be Spanish, wherever we met it. So also a traveller, with any experience in the composition of Spanish sermons and Spanish ollas, could make no mistake in respect of the following: *A sermon without Augustine is as a stew without bacon.*† Thus *Big and empty, like the Heidelberg tun,*‡ could have its home only in Germany; that enormous vessel, known as the Heidelberg tun, constructed to contain nearly 300,000 flasks, having now stood empty for hundreds of years. As regards, too, the following, *Not every parish-priest can wear*

* En casa del Moro no hables algarabia.

† Sermon sin Agostino, olla sin tocino.

‡ Gross und leer, wie das Heidelberger Fass.

Doctor Luther's shoes,* we could be in no doubt to what people it appertains. And this, *The world is a carcase, and they who gather round it are dogs*, plainly proclaims itself as belonging to those Eastern lands, where the unowned dogs prowling about the streets of a city are the natural scavengers, that would assemble round a carcase thrown in the way. So too the form which our own proverb, *Man's extremity, God's opportunity*, assumes among the Jews, namely this, *When the tale of bricks is doubled, Moses comes*,† plainly roots itself in the early history of that nation, being an allusion to Exod. v. 9–19, and without a knowledge of that history, would be unintelligible altogether

But while it is thus with some, which are bound by the very conditions of their existence to a narrow and peculiar sphere, or at all events move more naturally and freely in it than elsewhere, there are others, on the contrary, which we meet all the world over. True cosmopolites, they seem to have travelled from land to land, and to have made themselves a home equally in all. The Greeks obtained them probably from the older East, and again imparted them to the Romans; and from these they have found their way into all the languages of the western world.

Much, I think, might be learned from knowing

* Doctor Luther's Schuhe sind nicht allen Dorfpriestern gerecht.

† Cum duplicantur lateres, Moses venit.

what those truths are, which are so felt to be true by all nations, that all have loved to possess them in these compendious forms, wherein they may pass readily from mouth to mouth: which, thus cast into some happy form, have commended themselves to almost all people, and have become a portion of the common stock of the world's wisdom, in every land making for themselves a recognition and a home. Such a proverb, for instance, is *Man proposes, God disposes;** one which I am inclined to believe that every nation in Europe possesses, so deeply upon all men is impressed the sense of Hamlet's words, if not the words themselves:—

> "There's a divinity that *shapes* our ends,
> *Rough-hew* them how we will."

Sometimes the proverb does not actually in so many words repeat itself in various tongues. We have indeed exactly the same *thought*, but it takes an outward shape and embodiment, varying according to the various countries and periods in which it has been current; we have proverbs totally diverse from one another in their form and appearance, but which yet, when we look a little deeper into them, prove to be at heart one and the same, all these their differences being thus only, so to speak, variations of the same air. These are almost always an amusing, often an instructive, study; and to

* La gente pone, y Dios dispone.—Der Mensch denkt's; Gott lenkt's.

trace this likeness in difference has an interest lively enough. Thus the *forms* of the proverb, which brings out the absurdity of those reproving others for a defect or a sin, to whom the same cleaves in an equal or in a greater degree, have sometimes no visible connection at all, or the very slightest, with one another; yet, for all this, the proverb is at heart and essentially but one. We say in English: *The kiln calls the oven, "Burnt house;"* the Italians, *The pan says to the pot, "Keep off, or you'll smutch me;"** the Spaniards, *The raven cried to the crow, "Avaunt, blackamoor;"*† the Germans, *One ass nicknames another, "Long-ears;"*‡ while it must be owned there is a certain originality in the Catalan version of the proverb: *Death said to the man with his throat cut, "How ugly you look."* Under how rich a variety of forms does one and the same thought array itself here.

Let me quote another illustration of the same fact. We probably take for granted that *Coals to Newcastle* is a thoroughly English expression of the absurdity of sending to a place that which already abounds there—water to the sea, fagots to the wood—and English of course it is in the outward garment which it wears; but in its inner-

* La padella dice al pajuolo, Fatti in là, che tu mi tigni.

† Dijó la corneja al cuervo, Quítate allá, negro.

‡ Ein Esel schimpft den andern, Langohr.

most being it belongs to the whole world and to all times. Thus the Greeks said, *Owls to Athens*,* Attica abounding with these birds; the rabbis, *Enchantments to Egypt*, Egypt being of old esteemed the headquarters of all magic; the Orientals, *Pepper to Hindostan;* and in the Middle Ages they had this proverb, *Indulgences to Rome*—Rome being the centre and source of this spiritual traffic; and these by no means exhaust the list.

Let me adduce some other variations of the same descriptions, though not running through quite so many languages. Thus compare the German, *Who lets one sit on his shoulders, shall have him presently sit on his head*,† with the Italian, *If thou suffer a calf to be laid on thee, wtthin a little they'll clap on the cow;*‡ and again, with the Spanish, *Give me where I may sit down; I will make where I may lie down*.§ They all three plainly contain one and the same hint that undue liberties are best resisted at the outset, being otherwise liable to be followed up by other and greater ones; but this under how rich and humorous a variety of forms. Not very different are these that follow. We say: *Daub yourself with honey, and*

* Γλαῦκας εἰς 'Αθήνας.

† Wer sich auf der Achsel sitzen lässt, dem sitzt man nachher auf dem Kopfe.

‡ Se ti lasci metter in spalla il vitello, quindi a poco ti metteran la vacca.

§ Dame donde me asiente, que yo haró donde me acueste.

you'll be covered with flies—the Danes: *Make yourself an ass, and you'll have every man's sack on your shoulders*—while the French: *Who makes himself a sheep, the wolf devours him**—and the Persians: *Be not all sugar, or the world will swallow thee up;* to which they add, however, as its necessary complement, *nor yet all wormwood, or the world will spit thee out.*† Or again, we are content to say without a figure, *The receiver's as bad as the thief;* but the French, *He sins as much who holds the sack, as he who puts into it;*‡ and the Germans, *He who holds the ladder is as guilty as he who mounts the wall.*§ We say, *A stitch in time savs nine;* the Spaniards, *Who will not repair his gutter, repairs his whole house.*‖ We say, *Misfortunes never come single;* the Italians have no less than three proverbs to express the same popular conviction: *Blessed is that misfortune which comes single;* and again, *One misfortune is the vigil of another;* and again, *A misfortune and a friar are seldom alone.*¶ Or once more, the Russians say, *Call a peasant "Brother," he'll demand to be called "Father;"* the Italians, *Give a peasant*

* Qui se fait brebis, le loup le mange.

† There is a Catalan proverb to the same effect: Qui de tot es moll, de tot es foll.

‡ Autant pèche celui qui tient le sac, que celui qui met dedans.

§ Wer die Leiter hält, ist so schuldig wie der Dieb.

‖ Quien no adoba gotera, adoba casa entera.

¶ Benedetto è quel male, che vien solo.—Un mal è la vigilia dell'altro.—Un male ed un Frate di rado soli.

*your finger, he'll grasp your fist.** Many languages have this proverb, *God gives the cold according to the cloth;* † it is very beautiful, but attains not to the tender beauty of our own, *God tempers the wind to the shorn lamb.*

And, as in that last example, so not seldom will there be an evident superiority of a proverb in one language over one, which however resembles it closely in another. Moving in the same sphere, it will yet be richer, fuller, deeper. Thus our own, *A burnt child fears the fire*, is good; but that of many tongues, *A scalded dog fears cold water*, is better still. Ours does but express that those who have suffered once will henceforward be timid in respect of that same thing whence they have suffered; but that other the tendency to exaggerate such fears, so that now they shall fear even where no fear is. And the fact that so it will be, clothes itself in an almost infinite variety of forms. Thus one Italian proverb says: *A dog which has been beaten with a stick, is afraid of its shadow;* and another, which could only have had its birth in the sunny south, where the glancing but harmless lizard so often darts across our path: *Whom a serpent has bitten, a lizard alarms.*‡ With a little variation from this, the Jewish rabbis had said long

* Al villano, se gli porgi il dito, ei prende la mano.

† Dieu donne le froid selon le drap.—Cada cual siente el frio como anda vestido.

‡ Cui serpe mozzica, lucerta teme.

before: *One bitten by a serpent, is afraid of a rope's end;* even that which bears so remote a resemblance to a serpent as this does, shall now inspire him with terror; and the Cingalese, still expressing the same thought, but with imagery borrowed from their own tropic clime: *The man who has received a beating from a firebrand, runs away at sight of a firefly.*

Some of our Lord's sayings contain the same lessons which the proverbs of the Jewish rabbis contained already; for he was willing to bring forth even from his treasury things old as well as new; but it is very instructive to observe how they acquire in his mouth a dignity and decorum which, it may be, they wanted before. We are all familiar with that word in the Sermon on the mount, "Whosoever shall compel thee to go a mile, go with him twain." The rabbis had a proverb to match, lively and piquant enough, but certainly lacking the gravity of this, and which never could have fallen from the same lips: *If thy neighbor call thee an ass, put a packsaddle on thy back;* do not, that is, withdraw thyself from the wrong, but rather go forward to meet it. But thus, in least, as in greatest, it was his to make all things new.

Sometimes a proverb, without changing its shape altogether, will yet on the lips of different nations be slightly modified; and these modifications, slight as often they are, may not the less be eminently characteristic. Thus in English we say, *The river past, and God forgotten*, to express with how mournful a frequency, he whose assistance was invoked, it may have been earnestly, in the moment of peril, is remembered no more, so soon as by his help the danger has been surmounted. The Spaniards have the proverb too; but it is with them; *The river past, the saint forgotten*,* the saints being in Spain more prominent objects of invocation than God. And the Italian form of it sounds a still sadder depth of ingratitude: *The peril past, the saint mocked*;† the vows made to him in peril remaining unperformed in safety; and he treated something as, in Greek story, Juno was treated by Mandrabulus the Samian; who, having under her auspices and through her direction discovered a gold mine, in his instant gratitude vowed to her a golden ram; which he presently exchanged in intention for a silver one; and again this for a very small brass one; and this for nothing at all; the rapidly descending scale of whose gratitude, with the entire disappearance of his thank-offering, might very profitably live in our memories, as so perhaps it would be less likely to repeat itself in our lives.

* El rio pasado, el santo olvidado.

† Passato il punto, gabbato il santo.

LECTURE IV.

THE POETRY, WIT, AND WISDOM OF PROVERBS.

It will be my endeavor in the three lectures which I have still to deliver to justify the attention which I have claimed on behalf of proverbs from you, not merely by appealing to the authority of others, who at different times have prized and made much of them, but by bringing out and setting before you, so far as I have the skill to do it, some of the merits and excellencies by which they are mainly distinguished. Their wit, their wisdom, their poetry, the delicacy, the fairness, the manliness which characterize so many of them, their morality, their theology, will all by turns come under our consideration. Yet shall I beware of presenting them to you as though they embodied these nobler qualities only. I shall not keep out of sight that there are proverbs, course, selfish, unjust, cowardly, profane; "maxims" wholly undeserving of the honor implied by that name.* Still as my pleasure, and I doubt not yours, is rather with the

* Regulæ quæ inter *maximas* numerari merentur.

wheat than with the tares, I shall while I do not conceal this, prefer to dwell in the main on the nobler features which they present.

And first, in regard of the poetry of proverbs—whatever is *from* the people, or truly *for* the people, whatever either springs from their bosom, or has been cordially accepted by them, still more whatever unites both these conditions, will have poetry, imagination, in it. For little as the people's craving after wholesome nutriment of the imaginative faculty, and after an entrance into a fairer and more harmonious world than that sordid and confused one with which often they are surrounded, is duly met and satisfied, still they yearn after all this with an honest hearty yearning, which must put to shame the pallid indifference, the only affected enthusiasm of too many, whose opportunities of cultivating this glorious faculty have been so immeasurably greater than theirs. This being so, the proverbs being, as we have seen, the sayings that have found favor with the people, their peculiar inheritance, we may be quite sure that there will be poetry, imagination, passion, in them. So much we might affirm beforehand; our closer examination of them will confirm the confidence which we have been bold to entertain.

Thus we may expect to find that they will contain often bold imagery, striking comparisons; and such they do. Let serve as an example our own:

Gray hairs are death's blossoms;* or the Italian: *Time is an inaudible file*;† or the Greek: *Man a bubble*,‡ which Jeremy Taylor has expanded into such glorious poetry in the opening of the *Holy Dying*; or that Turkish: *Death is a black camel which kneels at every man's gate*; to take up, that is, the burden of a coffin there; or this Arabic one, on the never satisfied eye of desire: *Nothing but a handful of dust will fill the eye of man*; or another from the same quarter, worthy of Mecca's prophet himself, and of the earnestness with which he realized Gehenna, whatever else he may have come short in: *There are no fans in hell*; or this other, also from the east: *Hold all skirts of thy mantle extended, when heaven is raining gold*; improve, that is, to the uttermost the happier crises of thy spiritual life; or this one, current in the Middle Ages: *Whose life lightens, his words thunder*;§ or once more, this Chinese: *Towers are measured by their shadows, and great men by their calumniators*; however this last may have somewhat of an artificial air as tried by our standard of the proverb.

There may be poetry in a play upon words; and such we shall hardly fail to acknowledge in that

* In German: Grau' Hare sind Kirchkofsblumen.

† Il tempo è una lima sorda.

‡ Πομφόλυξ ὁ ἄνθρωπος.

§ Cujus vita fulgor, ejus verba tonitrua. Cf. Mark iii. 17: υἱοὶ βροντης.

beautiful Spanish proverb: *La verdad es siempre verde*, which I must leave in its original form; for were I to translate it, *The truth is always green*, its charm and chief beauty would be looked for in vain. It finds its pendant and complement in another, which I must also despair of adequately rendering: *Gloria vana florece, y no grana;* which would express this truth, namely, that vain glory can shoot up into stalk and ear, but can never attain to the full grain in the ear. Nor can we, I think, refuse the title of poetry to this eastern proverb, in which the wish that a woman may triumph over her enemies, clothes itself thus: *May her enemies stumble over her hair;*—may she flourish so, may her hair, the outward sign of this prosperity, grow so rich and long, may it so sweep the ground, that her detractors and persecutors may be entangled by it and fall.

And then, how exquisitely witty many proverbs are. Thus, not to speak of one familiar to us all, which is perhaps the queen of all proverbs: *The road to hell is paved with good intentions;** take this Scotch one: *A man may love his house well without riding on the ridge;* it is enough for a wise man to know what is precious to himself, without making himself ridiculous by evermore pro-

* Admirably glossed in the *Guesses at Truth:* "Pluck up the stones, ye sluggards, and break the devil's head with them."

claiming it to the world; or this of our own: *When the devil is dead, he never wants a chief mourner;* in other words, there is no abuse so enormous, no evil so crying, but that the interests or passions of some will be so bound up in its continuance that they will lament its extinction; or this Italian: *When rogues go in procession, the devil holds the cross;** when evil men have it thus far their own way, then worst is best, and in the inverted hierarchy which is then set up, the foremost in badness is foremost also in such honor as is going. Or consider this German one, in which the tender mercies of the feudal lords, of whom one is supposed to be speaking, are excellently parodied: *One must be too hard on the peasants;—hew off his hands and his feet.*† Or, take another from the same quarter, noting with slightest exaggeration a measure of charity which is only too common: *He will swallow an egg, and give away the shells in alms.*

The wit of proverbs spares few or none. They are, as may be supposed, especially intolerant of fools. *We* say: *Fools grow without watering;* no need therefore of adulation or flattery, to quicken them to a ranker growth; and the Russians: *Fools are not planted or sowed; they grow of themselves;* while the Spaniards: *If folly were a pain, there*

* Quando i furbi vanno in processione, il diavolo porta la croce.

† Der Bauer ist nit zu verderben: man hau' ihm denn Hand und Fuss ab.

*would be crying in every house;** having further an exquisitely witty one on learned folly as the most intolerable of all follies: *A fool, unless he knows Latin, is never a great fool.*† And here is excellently unfolded to us the secret of the fool's confidence: *Who knows nothing, doubts nothing.*‡

The shafts of their pointed satire are directed with an admirable impartiality against men of every degree, so that none of us will be found to have wholly escaped. To pass over those, and they are exceedingly numerous, which are aimed at members of the monastic orders,§ I must fain hope that this Bohemian one, pointing at the clergy, is not true; for it certainly argues no very forgiving temper on our parts in cases where we have been, or fancy ourselves to have been wronged. It is as follows: *If you have offended a clerk, kill him; else you never will have peace with him.*‖ And another proverb, worthy to take its place among the best even of the Spanish, charges the clergy with being the authors of the chiefest spiritual mischiefs which have arisen up in the church: *By the*

* Si la locura fuese dolores, en cada casa darian voces.

† Tonto, sin saber Latin, nunca es gran tonto.

‡ Qui rien ne sçait, de rien ne doute.

§ An earnest preacher of righteousness just before the Reformation quotes this one as current about them: Quod agere veretur obstinatus diabolus, intrepide agit reprobus et contumax monachus.

‖ It is Huss who, denouncing the sins of the clergy of this day, has preserved this proverb for us: Malum proverbium contra nos confinxerunt, dicentes, Si offenderis clericum, interfice eum; alias nunquam habebis pacem cum illo.

*vicar's skirts the devil climbs up into the belfry.** Nor do physicians appear in the Middle Ages to have been in very high reputation for piety; for a Latin medieval proverb boldly proclaims: *Where there are three physicians, there are two atheists.*† And as for lawyers, this of the same period, *Legista, nequista*,‡ expresses itself not with such brevity only, but with such downright plainness of speech, that I shall excuse myself from attempting to render it into English. Nor do other sorts and conditions of men escape. "The miller tolling with his golden thumb," has been often the object of malicious insinuations; and of him the Germans have a proverb: *What is bolder than a miller's neckcloth, which takes a thief by the throat every morning?*§ Evenhanded justice might perhaps require that I should find caps for other heads; and it is not that such are wanting, nor yet out of fear lest any should be offended, but only because I must needs hasten onward, that I leave this part of my subject without further development.

What a fine knowledge of the human heart will they often display. I know not whether this Persian saying on the subtleties of pride is a proverb in the very strictest sense of the word, but it is

* Por las haldas del vicario sube el diablo al campanario.

† Ubi tres Medici, duo Athei.

‡ In German: Juristen, bösen Christen.

§ Bebel: Dicitur in proverbio nostro; nihil esse audacius indusio molitoris, cum omni tempore matutino furem collo apprehendat.

forcibly uttered: *Thou shalt sooner detect an ant moving in the dark night on the black earth, than all the motions of pride in thine heart.* And on the wide reach of this sin the Italians say: *If pride were as art, how many graduates we should have;** and how excellent and searching is this word of theirs on the infinitely various shapes which this protean sin will assume: *There are who despise pride with a greater pride,*† one which might almost seem to have been founded on the story of Diogenes, who, treading under his feet a rich carpet of Plato's, exclaimed, "Thus I trample on the ostentation of Plato;" "With an ostentation of thine own," was the other's excellent retort;—even as on another occasion he observed, with admirable wit, that he saw the pride of the cynic peeping through the rents of his mantle: for indeed pride can array itself quite as easily in rags as in purple; can affect squalors as earnestly as splendors; the lowest place and the last is of itself no security at all for humility; and out of a sense of this *we* very well have said: *As proud go behind as before.*

Sometimes in their subtle observation of life, they arrive at conclusions which we would very willingly question or reject, but to which it is impossible to refuse a certain amount of assent. Thus it is with the very striking German proverb: *One*

* Se la superbia fosse arte, quanti Dottori avressimo.

† Tal sprezza la superbia con una maggior superbia.

*foe is too many; and a hundred friends too few.** There speaks out in this a sense of how much more *active* a principle in this world will hate be sometimes than love. The hundred friends will *wish* you well; but the one foe will *do* you ill. Their benevolence will be ordinarily passive; his malevolence will be constantly active; it will be *animosity*, or spiritedness in evil. The proverb will have its use, if we are stirred up by it to prove its assertion false, to show that, in very many cases at least, there is no such blot as it would set on the scutcheon of true friendship. In the same rank of unwelcome proverbs I must range this Persian one: *Of four things every man has more than he knows; of sins, of debts, of years, and of foes;* and this Spanish: *One father can support ten children; ten children can not support one father;* which, in so far as it rests upon a certain ground of truth, suggests a painful reflection in regard of the less strength which there must be in the filial than in the paternal affection, since to the one those acts of self-sacrificing love are easy, which to the other are hard, and often impossible. But yet, seeing that it is the order of God's providence in the world that fathers should in all cases support children, while it is the exception when children are called to support parents, one can only admire that wisdom which has made the instincts of natural affec-

* Ein Feind ist zu viel; und hundert Freunde sind zu wenig.

tion to run rather in the descending than in the ascending line; a wisdom to which this proverb, though with a certain exaggeration of the facts, bears witness.

How exquisitely delicate is the touch of this French proverb: *It is easy to go afoot when one leads one's horse by the bridle.** How fine and subtle an insight into the inner workings of the human heart is here; how many cheap humilities are here set at their true worth. It *is* easy to stoop from state, when that state may be resumed at will; easy for one to part with luxuries and indulgences, which he only parts with exactly so long as it may please himself. No reason, indeed, is to be found in this comparative easiness for the not 'going afoot;' on the contrary, it may be to him a most profitable exercise; but every reason for not esteeming the doing so too highly, nor setting it in value beside the trudging upon foot of him who has no horse to fall back on whatever moment he may please.

There is, and always must be, some rough work to be done in the world; work which, though rough, is not therefore, in the least, ignoble; and the schemes, so daintily conceived, of a luxurious society, which repose on a tacit assumption that nobody shall have to do this work, are touched with a fine irony in this Arabic proverb: *If I am*

* Il est aisé d'aller à pied, quand on tient son cheval par la bride.

master and thou art master, who shall drive the asses? *

Again, how clever is the satire of the following Haytien proverb, which, however, I must introduce with a little preliminary explanation. It was one current among the slave population of St. Domingo, and with it they ridiculed the ambition and pretension of the mulatto race immediately above them, who, in imitation of the French planters, must have their duels too — duels, however, which had nothing earnest or serious about them, invariably ending in a reconciliation and a feast, the kids which furnished the latter being in fact the only sufferers, their blood that which alone was shed. All this the proverb uttered: *Mulattoes fight, kids die.*†

And proverbs, witty in themselves, often become wittier still in their application, like gems that acquire new brilliancy from their setting, or from some novel light in which they are held. No writer that I know of has a happier skill in thus adding wit to the witty than Fuller, the church historian. Let me confirm this assertion by one or two examples drawn from his writings. He is describing the indignation, the outcries, the remonstrances, which the thousandfold extortions, the intolerable exac-

* The Galligan proverb, *You a lady, I a lady, who shall drive the hogs a-field?* (Vos dona, yo dona, quen botara a porca fora?) is only a variation of this.

† Mulates qua battent, cabrite qua morts.

tions of the papal see gave birth to in England during the reigns of such subservient kings as our Third Henry; yet he will not have his readers to suppose that the popes fared a whit the worse for all this outcry which was raised against them; not so, for *The fox thrives best when he is most cursed;** the very loudness of the clamor was itself rather an evidence how well they were faring. Or again, he is telling of that duke of Buckingham, well known to us through Shakespeare's *Richard the Third*, who, having helped the tyrant to a throne, afterward took mortal displeasure against him; this displeasure he sought to hide, till a season arrived for showing it with effect, in the deep of his heart, but in vain; for, as Fuller observes, *It is hard to halt before a cripple;* the arch-hypocrite Richard, he to whom dissembling was as a second nature, saw through and detected at once the shallow Buckingham's clumsier deceit. And the *Church History* abounds with similar happy applications. Fuller, indeed, possesses so much of the wit out of which proverbs spring, that it is not seldom difficult to tell whether he is adducing a proverb, or uttering some proverb-like saying of his own. Thus, I can not remember ever to have met any of the following, which yet sound like proverbs—the first on solitude as preferable to ill-companionship: *Better ride*

* A proverb of many tongues beside our own: thus in the Italian: Quanto più la volpe è maladetta, tanto maggior preda fa.

*alone than have a thief's company;** the second against certain who disparaged one whose excellencies they would have found it very difficult to imitate: *They who complain that Grantham steeple stands awry, will not set a straighter by it,*† and in this he warns against despising in any the tokens of honorable toil: *Mock not a cobbler for his black thumbs.*‡

But the glory of proverbs—that, perhaps, which strikes us most often and most forcibly in regard of them—is their shrewd common sense, the sound wisdom for the management of our own lives, and of our intercourse with our fellows, which so many of them contain. In truth, there is no region of practical life which they do not occupy, for which they do not supply some wise hints and counsels and warnings; there is hardly a mistake which in the course of our lives we have committed, but some proverb, had we known and attended to its lesson, might have saved us from it. "Adages," indeed, according to the more probable etymology of that word, they are—*apt for action* and use.§

Thus, how many of these popular sayings and what good ones there on the wisdom of governing the tongue: I speak not now of those urging the *duty*, though such are by no means wanting, but

* *Holy State*, B. 3, c. 5. † B. 2, c. 23. ‡ B. 3, c. 2.

§ Adagia, ad agendum apta; this is the etymology of the word given by Festus.

the wisdom, prudence, and profit, of knowing how to keep silence as well as how to speak. The Persian, perhaps, is familiar to many: *Speech is silvern, silence is golden;* with which we may compare the Italian, *He who speaks, sows; he who keeps silence, reaps:** and on the *safety* that is in silence, I know none happier than another from the same quarter, and one most truly characteristic: *Silence was never written down;*† while, on the other hand, we are excellently warned of the irrevocableness of the word which has once gone from us in this Eastern proverb: *Of thine unspoken word thou art master; thy spoken word is master of thee:* even as the same is set out elsewhere by many striking comparisons: it is the arrow from the bow, the stone from the sling; and, once launched, can as little be recalled as these.‡ Our own, *He who says what he likes, shall hear what he does not like*, gives a further motive for self-government in speech; and this Spanish is in a higher strain: *The evil which issues from thy mouth falls into thy bosom.*§ Nor is it enough to abstain ourselves from all such words; we must not make ourselves partakers in those of others, which it is only too easy to do; for,

* Chi parla semina, chi tace raccoglie.

† Il tacer non fù mai scritto.

‡ Palabra de boca, piedra de honda.—Palabra y piedra suelta no tiene vuelta.

§ El mal que de tu boca sale, en tu senso se cae.

as the Chinese have said very well: *He who laughs at an impertinence makes himself its accomplice.*

And then, in proverbs not a few, what profitable warnings have we against the fruits of evil companionship, as in that homely one of our own, *He that lies down with dogs, shall rise up with fleas;** or again, in the old Hebrew one, *Two dry sticks will set on fire one green;* or, in another from the East, which belongs to the same theme, and plainly shows whither such companionship will lead, *He that takes the raven for a guide, shall light upon carrion.*

What warnings do many contain against unreasonable expectations, against a looking for perfection in a world of imperfection, and generally a demanding of more from life than life can yield. We note very well the folly of one addicted to this, saying, *He expects better bread than can be made of wheat;* and the Portuguese, *He that will have a horse without fault, let him go a-foot.* Again, what a good word of caution in respect of the wisdom of considering oftentimes a step which, being once taken, is taken for ever, lies in the following Russian proverb: *Measure thy cloth ten times; thou canst cut it but once.* And in this Spanish the final isues of procrastination are well set forth: *By the street of "By-and-by," one arrives at the house of "Never."*† In how pleasant a way the avoiding

* Quien con perros se echa, con pulgas se levanta.

† Por la calle de despues se va à la casa de nunca.

of all appearance of evil is urged in the following Chinese: *In a field of melons tie not thy shoe; under a plum-tree adjust not thy cap.* And this Danish warns us well against relying too much on other men's silence, since there is no rarer gift than the capacity of keeping a secret: *Tell nothing to thy friend which thou wouldst not have thine enemy to know.* Here is a word which we owe to Italy, and which, laid to heart, might keep men out of lawsuits, or, being in them, from refusing to accept tolerable terms of accommodation: *The robes of lawyers are lined with the obstinacy of suitors.** Other words of wisdom and learning, for so I must esteem them, are these; this on the danger of being overset by prosperity: *Everything may be borne, except good fortune;*† with which may be compared our own, *Bear wealth, poverty will bear itself;* and another Italian, which says, *In prosperity no altars smoke.*‡ This is on the disgrace which will, sooner or later, follow upon dressing ourselves out in intellectual finery that does not belong to us: *Who arrays himself in other men's garments, they strip him in the middle of the street;*§ he is detected and laid bare, when and where detection is most shameful.

* Le vesti degl' avvocati sono fodraet dell' ostinazion dei litiganti.

† Ogni cosa si sopporta, eccetto il buon tempo.

‡ Nella prosperità non fumano g' altari.

§ Quien con ropa agena se viste, en la calle se queda encueros.

Of the same miscellaneous character, and derived from quarters the most diverse, but all of them of an excellent sense or shrewdness, are the following. This from Italy: *Who sees not the bottom, let him not pass the water.** This is current among the free blacks of Hayti: *Before crossing the river, do not curse the crocodile's mother:*† provoke not wantonly those in whose power you presently may be. This is Spanish: *Call me not "olive," till you see me gathered;*‡ being nearly parallel to our own, *Praise a fair day at night;* and this French, *Take the first advice of a woman, and not the second;*§ a proverb of much wisdom; for in processes of reasoning, out of which the second counsels would spring, women may and will be inferior to us; but in intuitions, in moral intuitions above all, they surpass us far; they have what Montaigne ascribes to them in a remarkable word, *l'esprit primesautier*, the leopard's spring, which takes its prey, if it be to take it at all, at the first bound.

And I can not but think, that, for as many as are seeking diligently to improve their time and opportunities of knowledge, with, at the same time, little

* Chi non vede il tondo, no passi l' acqua.

† Avant traversé rivier, pas juré maman caiman. This and one or two other Haytien proverbs quoted in this volume I have derived from a curious article, *Les mœurs et la litterature négres*, by Gustave D'Alaux, in the *Revue des deux Mondes*, Mai 15me, 1852.

‡ No me digas oliva, hasta que me veas cogida.

§ Prends le premier conseil d'une femme, et non le second.

of either which they can call their own, a very useful hint and warning against an error which lies very near, is contained in the little Latin proverb, *Compendia, dispendia.* Nor indeed for them only, but for all, and in numberless respects it often proves true that a short cut may be a very long way home; yet the proverb can never be applied better than to those little catechisms of science, those skeleton outlines of history, those epitomes of all useful information, those thousand delusive short-cuts to the attainment of that knowledge which can indeed only be acquired by them that travel on the king's highway—on the old, and as I must still call it, the royal road of patience, perseverance, and toil. Surely these *compendia*, so meager and so hungry, with little food for the intellect, with less for the affections, we may style with fullest right *dispendia*, wasteful as they generally prove of whatever time and labor and money is bestowed upon them.

And being on the subject of books and the choice of books, let me put before you a proverb, and in this reading age a very serious one; it comes to us from Italy, and it says, *There is no worse robber than a bad book.** Indeed, none worse, nor so bad; other robbers may spoil us of our money; but this one of our "goods"—of our time at any rate, even assuming the book to be only negatively bad; but

* Non v' è il peggior ladro d'un cattivo libro.

of how much more, of our principles, our faith, our purity of heart, supposing its badness to be positive, and not negative only.

Here are one or two prudent words on education. *A child may have too much of its mother's blessing;* yes, for that *blessing* may be no blessing, but rather a curse, if it take the shape of foolish and fond indulgence; and in the same strain is this German: *Better the child weep than the father.** And this, like many others, is found in so many tongues, that it can not be ascribed to one rather than another: *More springs in the garden than the gardener ever sowed.*† It is a proverb for many, but most of all for parents and teachers, that they lap not themselves in a false dream of security, as though nothing was at work or growing in the minds of the young in their guardianship, but what they themselves had sown there, as though there was not another who might very well have sown his tares beside and among any good seed of their sowing. At the same time the proverb has also its happier side. There may be, there often are, better things also in this garden than ever the earthly gardener set there, seeds of the more immediate sowing of God. In either of its aspects this proverb is one deserving to be laid to heart.

Proverbs will sometimes outrun and implicitly

* Es ist besser, das Kind weine denn der Vater.

† Nace en la huerta lo que no siembra el hortelano.

anticipate conclusions, which are only after long struggles and efforts arrived at as the formal and undoubted conviction of all thoughtful men. After how long a conflict has that been established as a maxim in political economy, which the brief Italian proverb long ago announced: *Gold's worth is gold.** What millions upon millions of national wealth have been as good as thrown into the sea, from the inability of those who have had the destinies of nations in their hands to grasp this simple proposition, that everything which could purchase money, or which money would fain purchase, was as really wealth as the money itself. What forcing of national industries into unnatural channels has resulted from this! what mischievous restrictions in the buying and selling of one people with another! Nay, can the truth which this proverb affirms be said even now to be accepted without gainsaying—so long as the talk about the balance of trade being in favor of or against a nation, as the fear of draining a country of its gold, still survive?

Here is a proverb of many tongues: *One sword keeps another in its scabbard;** surely a far wiser and far manlier word than the puling yet mischievous babble of our shallow peace societies, which,

* Oro è, che oro vale; and of the multitudes that are rushing to the Australian gold-fields, some may find this also true: Più vale guadagnar in loto che perder in oro.

* Una spada tien l' altra nel fodro.

while they fancy that they embody, and they only embody, the true spirit of Christianity, proclaim themselves in fact ignorant of all which it teaches; for they dream of having peace the fruit, while at the same time the root of bitterness out of which have grown all the wars and fightings that have ever been in the world, namely the lusts which stir in men's members, remain strong and vigorous as ever. But no; it is not they that are the peace-makers: in the face of an evil world, and of a world determined to continue in its evil, *He who bears the sword*—and though he fain would not, yet knows how, if need be, to wield it—*bears peace.**

Let me add another proverb, bearing on a subject which is occupying all patriot hearts in England at this present time: *Far-off water will not quench near fire.*† They who watch, and are answerable to their fellow-countrymen, for the safety of this our beloved land, and not for its safety only, but the inviolated honor of its shores, have laid to heart, if not the proverb, yet at all events the truth which it embodies, having resolved that an English fleet shall guard our English coasts. And this is well; for let us only suppose that a blow were struck at this mighty's empire's heart, at the home and sanctuary of its greatness—no improbable supposition, when force and fraud are met together, and are

* Qui porte épée, porte paix.

† Acqua lontana non spegne fuoco vicino.

watching their opportunity to strike it—what profit would it then be that the mighty armaments of England covered the distant seas, that her soldiers were winning comparatively barren victories in Africa and the East? The *far-off water*, as this proverb warns us, would altogether be useless for quenching the near fire.

One of the most remarkable features of a good proverb is the singular variety of applications which it will admit, which indeed it challenges and invites. Not lying on the surface of things, but going deep down to their heart, it will be found capable of being applied again and again, under circumstances the most different; like the gift of which Solomon spake, "whithersoever it turneth, it prospereth;" or like a diamond cut and polished upon many sides, which reflects and refracts the light upon every one. There can be no greater mistake than the attempt to tie it down and restrict it to a single application, when indeed the very character of it is that it is ever finding or making new ones for itself.

It is nothing strange that, with words of Eternal Wisdom, this should be so, and, in respect of them, my assertion can not need a proof. I will, notwithstanding, adduce as a first confirmation of it a scriptural proverb, one which fell from the Lord's lips in his last prophecies about Jerusalem, *Wheresoever the carcase is, there will the eagles be gathered together* (Matt. xxiv. 28), and which probably he had taken up from Job xxxix. 30. Who would venture to say that he had exhausted the meaning of this wonderful saying? For is it not properly inexhaustible? All history is a comment on these words. Wherever there is a church or a people abandoned by the spirit of life, and so a carcase, tainting the atmosphere of God's moral world, around it assemble the ministers and messengers of Divine justice, "the eagles" (or vultures, more strictly, for the true eagle does not feed on aught but what itself has slain), the scavengers of God's moral world, scenting out as by a mysterious instinct the prey from afar, and charged to remove presently the offence out of the way. This proverb, for the saying has passed upon the lips of men, and thus has become such, is being fulfilled evermore. The wicked Canaanites were the carcase, when the children of Israel entered into their land, the commissioned eagles that should remove them out of sight. At a later day the Jews were themselves the carcase, and the Romans the eagles; and when, in the progress of decay, the Roman empire had quite lost the spirit of life, and those virtues of the family and the nation which had deservedly made it great, the northern tribes, the eagles now, came down upon it, to tear it limb from limb, and make room for a new creation that should grow up in its stead. Again, the Persian empire was the carcase; Alexander and his Macedonian hosts the eagles that by unerring instinct gathered round it to complete its doom. The Greek church in the seventh century was too nearly a carcase to escape the destiny of such, and the armies of Islam scented their prey, and divided it among them. In modern times, Poland was, I fear, such a carcase; and this one may affirm, without in the least extenuating their guilt who partitioned it; for it might have been just for it to suffer, what yet it was most unrighteous for others to inflict. Nay, where do you not find an illustration of this proverb, from such instances on the largest scale as these, down to that of the silly and profligate heir, surrounded by sharpers and blacklegs, and preyed on by these? Everywhere it is true that *Wheresoever the carcase is, there will the eagles be gathered together.*

Or, again, consider such a proverb as the short but well-known one, *Extremes meet.* Short as it is, it is yet a motto on which whole volumes might be written, which is finding its illustration every day, in small and in great, in things trivial and in things most important, in the histories of single men, and in those of nations and of churches. Consider some of its every-day fulfilments—old age ending in second childhood; cold performing the effects of heat, and scorching as heat would have done; the extremities of joy and of grief alike finding utterance in tears; the second singular "thou" instead of the plural "you," employed in so many languages to inferiors and to God, never to equals; just as servants and children are alike called by the Christian name, but not those who stand in the midway of intimacy between them. Or to take some further illustrations from the moral world, of extremes meeting; observe how often those who begin their lives as spendthrifts end them as misers; how often the flatterer and the calumniator meet in the same person; out of a sense of which the Italians say well, *Who paints me before, blackens me behind;** observe how those who yesterday would have sacrificed to Paul as a god will to-day stone him as a malefactor (Acts xiv. 18, 19: cf. xxviii. 4–6); even as Roman emperors would one day have blasphemous honors paid to them by the populace, and the next their bodies would be dragged by a hook through the streets of the city, to be flung into the common sewer. Or note again in what close alliance hardness and softness, cruelty and self-indulgence ("lust hard by hate"), are continually found; or in law, how the *summum jus*, where unredressed by equity, becomes the *summa injuria*, as in the case of Shylock's pound of flesh, which was indeed no more than was in the bond. Or observe on a greater scale, as lately in France, how a wild and lawless democracy may be transformed by the base trick of a conjuror into an atrocious military tyranny.†

* Chi dinanzi mi pinge. di dietro mi tinge.

† How and why it is that extremes here meet, and what are the

Or read thoughtfully the history of the church and of the sects, and you will not fail to note what things apparently the most remote are yet in the most fearful proximity with one another: how often, for example, a false ascetism has issued in frantic outbreaks of fleshly lusts, and those who avowed themselves at one time ambitious to live lives above men, have ended in living lives below beasts. Again, take note of England at the Restoration exchanging all in a moment the sour strictness of the puritans for a license and debauchery unknown to it before. Or, once more, consider the exactly similar position in respect of scripture, taken up by the Romanists on the one side, the quakers and familists on the other. Seeming, and in much being, so remote from one another, they yet have this fundamental in common, that scripture, insufficient in itself, needs a supplement from without, those finding it in a pope, and these in what they call the "inward light." With these examples before you, not to speak of the many others which might be adduced,* you will own, I think, that this proverb, *Extremes meet*—or its parallel, *Too far east is west*—reaches very far into the heart of things: and with this, for the present, I must conclude.

inner affinities between a democracy and a tyranny, Plato has wonderfully traced (*Rep.* ii. p. 217).

* "*Extremes meet.* Truths, of all others the most awful and interesting, are too often considered as *so* true, that they lose all the power of truths, and lie, bedridden in the dormitory of the soul, side by side with the most despised and exploded errors."—*Coleridge, Aids, &c.*

LECTURE V.

THE MORALITY OF PROVERBS.

THE morality of proverbs is a subject which I have not been able to leave wholly untouched until now, for of necessity it has offered itself to us continually, in one shape or another; yet hitherto I have not regularly dealt with or considered it. To it I propose to devote the present lecture. But how, it may be asked at the outset, can any general verdict be pronounced about them? In a family like theirs, spread so widely over the face of the earth, are there not to be found worthy members and unworthy, proverbs noble and base, holy and profane, heavenly and earthly;—yea, heavenly, earthly, and devilish? What common judgment of phrase or censure can be pronounced on all these? Evidently none. The only question, therefore, for our consideration must be, whether there exists any such large and unquestionable preponderance either of the better sort or of the worse, as shall give us a right to pronounce a judgment on the whole in their favor or against them, to affirm of them that their prevailing influence and weight are thrown into the balance of the good or of the evil.

And here I am persuaded that no one can have devoted any serious attention to this aspect of the subject, but will own (and seeing how greatly popular morals are affected by popular proverbs, will own with thankfulness), that, if not without serious exceptions, yet still in the main they range themselves under the banners of the right and of the truth; he will allow that of so many as move in an ethical sphere at all, very far more are children of light and the day than of darkness and night. Indeed, the comparative paucity of unworthy proverbs is a very noticeable fact, and one to the causes of which I shall have presently to recur.

At the same time, when I affirm this, I find it necessary to make certain explanations, to draw certain distinctions. In the first place, I would not in so saying, in the least deny that an ample number of coarse proverbs are extant: it needs but to turn over a page or two of Ray's *Collection of English Proverbs*, or indeed of any collection in any tongue, which has not been weeded carefully, to convince oneself of the fact; nor yet would I deny,that of these many may, more or less, live on the lips of men. Having their birth, for the most part, in a period of a nation's literature and life when men are much more plain-spoken, and have far fewer reticences than is afterward the case, it is nothing strange that some of them, employing words forbidden now, but not forbidden then, should sound coarse and indelicate enough in our ears: while indeed there are others, whose offence and grossness these considerations, while they may mitigate, are quite insufficient to excuse. But at the same time, gross words and images (I speak not of wanton ones), bad as they may be, are altogether different from immoral maxims and rules of life. And it is these immoral maxims, unrighteous, selfish, or otherwise unworthy rules, of which I would affirm the number to be, if not absolutely, yet relatively small.

And then further, in estimating the morality of proverbs, this also will claim in justice not to be forgotten. In the same manner as coarse proverbs are not necessarily immoral, so the application which is made of a proverb by us may very often be hardhearted and selfish, while yet the proverb itself is very far from so being. This selfishness and hardness lay not in it of primary intention, but only by our abuse; and in the cases of several, these two things, the proverb itself, and the ordinary employment of it, will demand to be kept carefully apart from one another. For instance: *He has made his bed, and now he must lie on it; As he has brewed, so he must drink; As he has sown, so must he reap;** if these are employed to justify

* They have for their Latin equivalents such as these: Colo quod

us in refusing to save others, so far as we may, from the consequences of their own folly, or imprudence, or even guilt, why then one can only say that they are very ill employed: and there are few of us with whom it would not have gone hardly, had all those about us acted in the spirit of these proverbs so misinterpreted; had they refused to mitigate for us, so far as they could, the consequences of our errors. But if the words are taken in their true sense, as homely announcements of that law of divine retaliations in the world, according to which men shall eat of the fruit of their own doings, and be filled with their own ways, who shall gainsay them? What affirm they more than every page of Scripture, every turn of human life, is affirming too, namely, that the everlasting order of God's universe can not be violated with impunity, that there is a continual returning upon men of what they have done, and that in their history we may read their judgment.

Charity begins at home, is the most obvious and familiar of these proverbs, selfishly abused. It may be, no doubt it often is, made the plea for a selfish withholding of assistance from all but a few, whom men may include in their "at home," while sometimes the proverb receives a narrower interpretation still, and self and self only, is accounted

aptâsti, ipsi tibi nendum est;—Ut sementem feceris, ita metes;—Qui vinum bibit, fæcem bibat.

to be "at home." And yet, in truth, what were that charity worth, which did not begin at home, which did not preserve the divine order and proportion and degree? Not for nothing have we been grouped in families, neighborhoods, and nations; and he who will not recognise the divinely appointed nearnesses to himself of some over others, who thinks to be a cosmopolite without being a patriot, a philanthropist without owning a distinguishing love for them that are peculiarly "his own," who would thus have a circumference without a centre, deceives his own heart, and affirming all men to be equally dear to him, is indeed affirming them to be equally indifferent. Home, the family, this is as the hearth at which the affections which are afterward to go forth and warm in a larger circle, are themselves to be kept lively and warm; and the charity which did not exercise itself in outcomings of kindness and love in the narrower, would be little likely to seek a wider range for itself. Wherever else it may *end*, and the larger the sphere which it makes for itself the better, it must yet *begin* at home.*

There are, again, proverbs which, from another point of view, might seem of an ignoble cast, and

* In respect of other proverbs, such as the following, Tunica pallio propior;—Frons occipitio prior;—I have greater doubt. The misuse lies nearer; the selfishness may very probably be in the proverb itself, and not in our application of it; though even these seem not incapable of a fair interpretation.

as calculated to lower the tone of morality among those that received them; proposing as they do secondary, and therefore unworthy, motives to actions, which ought to be performed out of the highest. I mean such as this: *Honesty is the best policy;* wherein honesty is commended, not because it is right, but because it is most prudent and politic, and has the promise of this present world. Now doubtless there are proverbs not a few which, like this, move in the region of what has been well called "prudential morality;" and did we accept them as containing the whole circle of motives to honesty or other right conduct, nothing could be worse, or more fitted to lower the moral standard of our lives. He who resolves to be honest because, and only because, it is *the best policy*, will be little likely long to continue honest at all. But the proverb does not pretend to usurp the place of an ethical rule; it does not presume to cast down the higher law which should determine to honesty and uprightness, that it may put itself in its place; it only declares that honesty, let alone that it is the right thing, is also, even for this present world, the wisest. Nor dare we, let me further add, despise prudential morality, such as is embodied in sayings like this. The motives which it suggests are helps to a weak and tempted virtue, may prove great assistances to it in some passing moment of a violent temptation, however little they can be regarded as able to make men *for a continuance* even outwardly upright and just.

And once more, proverbs are not to be accounted selfish, which announce selfishness; unless they do it either avowedly recommending it as a rule and maxim of life, or, if not so, yet with an evident complacency and satisfaction in the announcement which they make, and in this more covert and perhaps still more mischievous way, taking part with the evil which they proclaim. There are a great many proverbs, which a lover of his race would be very thankful if there had been nothing in the world to justify or to provoke; for the convictions they embody, the experiences on which they rest must be regarded as very far from complimentary to human nature; but seeing that there is, it would be idle to wish them away, to wish that this evil had not found its utterance. Nay, it is much better that it should so have done; for thus taking form and shape, and being brought directly under notice, it may be better watched against and avoided.

Such proverbs, not selfish, but rather detecting selfishness and laying it bare, are the following; this Russian, on the only too slight degree in which we are touched with other men's troubles: *The burden is light on the shoulders of another;* with which the French may be compared: *One has always enough strength to bear the misfortunes of* *one's friends.** Such is this Italian: *Every one draws the water to his own mill;*† or as it appears in its Eastern shape, which brings up the desert-bivouac before one's eyes: *Every one rakes the embers to his own cake;* such this Latin, on the comparative wastefulness wherewith that which is another's is too often used: *Men cut broad thongs from other men's leather;*‡ with many more of the same character, which it would be only too easy to bring together.

With all this, I would not of course in the least deny that immoral proverbs, and only too many of them, exist. For if they are, as we have recognised them to be, the genuine transcript of what is stirring in the hearts, and uttering itself by the lips, of men, then, since there is cowardice, untruth, selfishness, unholiness, profaneness, there, how should they be wanting here? The world is not so consummate a hypocrite as the entire absence of all such would imply. There will be proverbs merely selfish, as our own; *Every one for himself, and God for us all;* or as this Dutch: *Self's the man;** or more shamelessly cynical still, as the French;

* On a toujours assez de force pour supporter le malheur de ses amis. I confess this sounds to me rather like an imitation of Rochefoucault than a genuine proverb.

† Ognun tira l'acqua al suo molino.

‡ Ex alieno tergore lata secantur lora.

§ Zelf is de Man.

Better a grape for me, than two figs for thee;* or such as proclaim a doubt and disbelief in the existence of any high moral integrity anywhere, as *Every man has his price*; or assume that poor men can scarcely be honest, as *It is hard for an empty sack to stand straight*; or take it for granted that every man would cheat every other if he could, as the French: *Count after your father*;† or, if they do not actually "speak good of the covetous," yet assume it possible that any blessing can wait on that which a wicked covetousness has heaped together, as the Spanish: *Blessed is the son whose father went to the Devil*; or find cloaks and apologies for sin, as the German: *Once is never*;‡ or such as would imply that the evil of a sin lay not in its sinfulness, but in the outward disgrace annexed to it, as the Italian: *A sin concealed is half forgiven*.§ Or again there will be proverbs dastardly and base, as the Spanish maxim of caution, which advises to *Draw the snake from its hole by another man's hand*; to put, that is, another, and it may be for your own profit, to the peril from which you shrink yourself; or more dastardly still,

* J'aime mieux un raisin pour moi que deux figues pour toi.

† Comptez après votre père. Compare the Spanish: Entre dos amigos un notario y dos testigos.

‡ Einmal, keinmal. This proverb was turned to such bad uses, that a German divine thought it necessary to write a treatise against it. There exist indeed several old works in German with such titles as the following, *Ungodly Proverbs and their Refutation.*

§ Peccato celato, mezzo perdonato.

"scoundrel maxims," an old English poet has called them; as for instance, that one which is acted on only too often: *One must howl with the wolves;** in other words, when a general cry is raised against any, it is safest to join in it, lest one be supposed to sympathize with its object; he must howl with the wolves, who would not be hunted by them. In the whole circle of proverbs I know no baser, nor more dastardly than this. And yet who will say that he has never traced in himself the cowardly temptation to obey it? And there will be, of which I shall spare you any examples, proverbs wanton and impure, and not merely proverbs thus earthly and sensual, but devilish; such as some of those Italian on revenge which I quoted in my third lecture.

But for all this these immoral proverbs, rank weeds among the wholesome corn, are comparatively rare. In the minority with all people, they are immeasurably in the minority with most. The fact is not a little worthy of our note. Surely there lies in it a solemn testimony, that however men may and do in their conduct continually violate the rule of right, yet these violations are ever felt to be such, are inwardly confessed not to be the law of man's life, but the transgressions of the law; and thus, stricken as with a secret shame, and paying an unconscious homage to the majesty of

* Badly turned into a rhyming pentameter:—

Consonus esto lupis, cum quibus esse cupis.

goodness, they do not presume to raise themselves into maxims, nor for all the frequency with which they may be repeated pretend to claim recognition as abiding standards of action.

As the sphere in which the proverb moves is no imaginary world, but that actual and often very homely world which is round us and about us—as it does not float in the clouds, but sets its feet firmly on this common earth of ours from which itself once grew, being occupied with present needs and every-day cares—it is only natural that the proverbs having reference to money should be numerous; and in the main it would be well if the practice of the world rose to the height of its convictions as expressed in these. Frugality is connected with so many virtues—at least, its contrary makes so many impossible—that the numerous proverbial maxims inculcating this, than which none perhaps are more frequent on the lips of men, must be regarded as belonging to the better order; especially when taken with the check of others, which forbid this frugality from degenerating into a sordid and dishonorable parsimony; such, I mean, as our own; *The groat is ill saved which shames its master.* In how many the conviction speaks out that the hastily-gotten will hardly be the honestly-gotten, that "he who makes haste to be rich shall not be innocent," as when the Spaniards say: *He who will* *be rich in a year, at the half-year they hang him;** in how many others, the confidence that the ill-won will also be the ill-spent,† that he who shuts up unlawful gain in his storehouses, is shutting up a fire that will one day destroy them. Very solemn and weighty in this sense is the German proverb: *The unrighteous penny corrupts the righteous pound;*‡ and the Spanish, too, is striking: *That which is another's always yearns for its lord;* § it yearns, that is to be gone and get to its true owner. In how many the conviction is expressed that this mammon, which more than anything else men are tempted to think God does not concern himself about, is yet given and taken away by him according to the laws of his righteousness; given sometimes to his enemies and for their greater punishment, that under its fatal influence they may grow worse and worse, for *The more the carle riches, he wretches;* but oftener withdrawn, because no due acknowledgment of him was made in its use; as when the German proverb declares: *Charity gives itself rich; covetousness hoards itself poor;*‖ and the Danish: *Give alms, that thy*

* Quien en un año quiere ser rico, al medio le ahorcan.

† Male parta male dilabuntur.—Wie gewonnen, so zerronnen.

‡ Ungerechter Pfennig verzehrt gerechten Thaler.

§ Lo ageno siempre pia por su dueño.

‖ Der Geiz sammlet sich arm, die Milde giebt sich reich. In the sense of the latter half of this proverb, we say, *Drawn wells are seldom dry;* though this word is capable of very far wider application.

children may not ask them; and the rabbis, with a yet deeper significance: *Alms are the salt of riches;* the true antiseptic, which as such shall prevent them from themselves corrupting, and from corrupting those that have them; which shall hinder them from developing a germ of corruption, such as shall in the end involve in one destruction them and their owners.* At the same time, as it is the very character of proverbs to look at matters all round, there are others to remind that even this very giving itself shall be with forethought and discretion; thus there is a Danish which says, *So give to-day, that thou shalt be able to give to-morrow;* and another: *So give to one, that thou shalt have to give to another.*†

Let me further invite you to observe and to ad-

* There is one remarkable Latin proverb on the moral cowardliness which it is the character of riches to generate, saying more briefly the same which Wordsworth said when he proclaimed—

"That riches are akin
To fear, to change, to cowardice, and death;"

it is this: Timidus Plutus; and has sometimes suggested to me the question whether he might not have had it in his mind when he composed his great sonnet in prospect of the invasion:—

"These times touch moneyed worldlings with dismay;"

not that his genius needed any such solicitation from without; for the poem is only the natural outgrowth of that spirit and temper in which the whole series of noble and ennobling poems, the *Sonnets to Liberty,* is composed, and in perfect harmony with the rest; yet is it, notwithstanding, in a very wonderful way shut up in the two words of the ancient proverb.

† Giv saa i Dag, at du og kandst give i morgen.—Giv een at du kand give en anden.

mire the prevailing tone of manliness which pervades the great body of the proverbs of all nations: let me urge you to take note how very few there are which would fain persuade you that "luck is all," or that your fortunes are in any other hands, under God, than your own. There are some, but they are exceptions, to which the gambler, the idler, the so-called "waiter upon Providence," can appeal. For the most part, however, they courageously accept the law of labor, *No pains, no gains; No sweat, no sweet; No mill, no meal*,* as the appointed law and condition of man's life. *Where wilt thou go, ox, that thou wilt not have to plough?*† is the Catalan remonstrance, addressed to one who imagines by any outward change of circumstances to evade the inevitable task and toil of existence. And this is Turkish: *It is not with saying, Honey, honey, that sweetness will come into the mouth;* and to many languages another with its striking image, *Sloth, the key of poverty*,‡ belongs; while, on the other hand, there are in almost all tongues such proverbs as the following: *God helps them that help themselves;*§ or, as it appears with a slight

* This is the English form of that worthy old classical proverb: *Φεύγων μύλον, ἄλφιτα φεύγει*, or in Latin: Qui vitat molam, vitat farinam.

† Ahont anirás, bou, que no llaures? I prefer this form of it to the Spanish: Adonde yrá el buey, que no are?

‡ Pereza, llave de pobreza.

§ Dii facientes adjuvant.

variation in the Basque, *God is a good worker, but he loves to be helped.* And these proverbs, let me observe by the way, were not strange, in their import at least, to the founder of that religion which is usually supposed to inculcate a blind and indolent fatalism—however some who call themselves by his name may have forgotten the lesson which they convey. Certainly they were not strange to Mahomet himself, if the following excellently-spoken word has been rightly ascribed to him. One evening, we are told, after a weary march through the desert, he was camping with his followers, and overheard one of them saying, "I will loose my camel and commit it to God;" on which Mahomet took him up: "Friend, *tie* thy camel, and commit it to God;"* do, that is, whatever is thine to do, and then leave the issue in higher hands; but till thou hast done this, till thou hast thus helped thyself, thou hast no right to look to Heaven to help thee.

How excellently this unites genuine modesty and manly self-assertion: *Sit in your own place, and no man can make you rise;* and how good is this Spanish, on the real dignity which there often is in doing things for ourselves, rather than in standing by and suffering others to do them for us: *Who has a mouth, let him not say to another, Blow.*†

* According to the Spanish proverb: Quien bien ata, bien desata.

† Quien tiene boca, no diga á otro, Sopla.

And as a part of this, which I have called the manliness of proverbs, let me especially note the noble utterances which so many contain, summoning to a brave encountering of adverse fortune, to perseverance under disappointment and defeat, and a long-continued inclemency of fate. *Where one door shuts, another opens;** this belongs to too many nations to allow of our ascribing it especially to any one. And this Latin, *The sun of all days has not yet gone down,*† however, in its primary application, intended for those who are at the top of Fortune's wheel, to warn them that they be not high-minded — for there is yet time for many a revolution in that wheel—is equally good for those at the bottom, and as it contains warning for those, so strength and encouragement for these; for, as the Italians say, *The world is his who has patience.*‡ And then, to pass over some of our own, so familiar that they need not be adduced, how manful a lesson is contained in this Persian proverb: *A stone that is fit for the wall is not left in the way.* It is a saying made for them who appear for a while to be overlooked, neglected, passed by; who perceive in themselves capacities, which as yet no one else has recognised or cared to turn to account. Only *be fit for the wall;* square,

* Donde una puerta se cierra, otra se abre.
† Nondum omnium dierum sol occidit.
‡ Il mondo è, di chi ha pazienza.

polish, prepare thyself for it; do not limit thyself to the bare acquisition of such knowledge as is absolutely necessary for thy present position; but rather learn languages, acquire useful information, stretch thyself out on this side and on that, cherishing and making much of whatever aptitudes thou findest in thyself; and it is certain thy turn will come. Thou wilt not be *left in the way;* sooner or later the builders will be glad of thee; the wall will need thee to fill up a place in it, quite as much as thou needest a place to occupy in the wall. For the amount of real capacity in this world is so small, that places want persons to fill them quite as really as persons want to fill places; although it must be allowed, they are not always as much aware of their want.

And this proverb, Italian and Spanish, *If I have lost the ring, yet the fingers are still here,** is another of these brave utterances of which I have been speaking. In it is asserted the comparative indifference of that loss which reaches but to things external to us, so long as we ourselves remain, and are true to ourselves. *The fingers* are far more than *the ring:* if indeed those had gone, then *the man* would have been maimed; but another ring may come for that which has disappeared, or even with none the fingers will be fingers still. And as

* Se ben ho perso l'anello, ho pur anche le ditta;—Si se perdieron los anillos, aqui quedaron los dedillos.

at once a contrast and complement to this, take another, current among the free blacks of Hayti, and expressing well the little profit which there will be to a man in pieces of mere good luck, which are no true outgrowths of anything which is in him; the manner in which, having no root in himself out of which they grew, they will, as they came to him by hazard, go from him by the same: *The knife which thou hast found in the highway, thou wilt lose in the highway.**

But these numerous proverbs, urging self-reliance, bidding us first to aid ourselves, if we would have Heaven to aid us, must not be dismissed without a word or two at parting. Prizing them, as we well may, and the lessons which they contain, at the highest, yet it will be profitable for us, at the same time, always to remember that to such there lies very near such a mischievous perversion as this: "Aid thyself, and thou wilt need no other aid;" even as they have been sometimes, no doubt, understood in this sense. As, then, the pendant and counter-weight to them all, not as unsaying what they have said, but as fulfilling the other hemisphere in the complete orb of truth, let me remind you of such also as the following, often quoted or alluded to by Greek and Latin authors:

* In their bastard French it runs thus: Gambette ous trouvé nen gan chimin, nen gan chimin ous va pèdè li. It may have been originally French, at any rate the French have a proverb very much to the same effect: Ce qui vient par la flute, s'en va par le tambour.

The net of the sleeping (fisherman) takes;* a proverb the more interesting, that we should have in the words of the Psalmist (Ps. cxxvii. 2), were they accurately translated, a beautiful and perfect parallel: "He giveth his beloved" (not "sleep," as in our version, but) "in their sleep;" his gifts gliding into their bosoms, they knowing not how, and as little expecting as having labored for them. Of how many of the best gifts of every man's life will he not thankfully acknowledge this to have been true; or, if he refuse, and will acknowledge no *eudæmonia*, no "favorable providence," in his prosperities, but will see them all as of work, how little he deserves, how little likely he is, to retain them to the end. Let us hold fast, then, this proverb, as the most needful complement of those.

I feel that I should be wanting to hearers such as those who are assembled here, that I should fail in that purpose which has been, more or less, present to me even in dealing with the lighter portions of my subject, if I did not earnestly remind you of the many of these sayings that there are, which, while they have their lesson for all, yet seem more directly addressed to those standing, as not a few

* Εὕδοντι κύρτος αἱρεῖ.—Dormienti rete trahit. The reader with a *Plutarch's Lives* within his reach, may turn to the very instructive little history told in connection with this proverb, of Timotheus the Athenian commander; a history which only requires to be translated into Christian language to contain a deep moral for all.—(*Sulla*, c. 6.)

6

of us here, at the threshold of the more serious and earnest portion of their lives. Lecturing to a *Young Men's Society*, I shall not unfitly press these upon your notice. Take this Italian one, for instance: *When you grind your corn, give not the flour to the devil, and the bran to God;* in the distribution, that is, of your lives, apportion not your best years, your strength, and your vigor, to the service of sin and of the world, and only the refuse and rejected to your Maker—the wine to others, and the lees only to him. Not so; for there is another ancient proverb,* which we have made very well our own, and which in English runs thus, *It is too late to spare when all is spent.* The words have obviously a primary application to the goods of this present life; it is ill saving here, when nothing, or next to nothing, is left to save. But they are applied well by a heathen moralist (and the application lies very near) to those who begin to husband precious time, and to live for life's true ends, when life is nearly gone, is now at its dregs; for, as he well urges, it is not the least only which remains at the bottom, but the worst.† On the other hand, *The morning hour has gold in its mouth;*‡ and this, true in respect of each of our

* Sera in imo parsimonia.

† Seneca (*Ep.* i.): Non enim tantum *minimum* in imo, sed *pessimum* remanet.

‡ Morgenstund' hat Gold im Mund.

days, in which the earlier hours given to toil will yield larger and more genial returns than the later, is true in a yet higher sense, of that great life-day, whereof all the lesser days of our life make up the moments — is true in respect of moral no less than mental acquisition. The *evening* hours have often only *silver* in their mouths at the best. Nor is this Arabic proverb, as it appears to me, other than a very solemn one, being far deeper than at first sight it might seem: *Every day in thy life is a leaf in thy history* — a leaf which shall once be turned back to again, that it may be seen what was written there; and that whatever *was* written may be read out in the hearing of all.

And among the proverbs having to do with a prudent ordering of our lives from the very first, this Spanish seems well worthy to be adduced: *That which the fool does in the end, the wise man does at the beginning;** the wise with a good grace what the fool with an ill; the one to much profit what the other to little or to none. A word worth laying to heart; for, indeed, that purchase of the Sibylline books by the Roman king, what a significant symbol it is of that which at one time or another, or, it may be, at many times, is finding place in almost every man's life; the same thing to be done in the end, the same price to be païd at the last, with only the difference, that much of the ad-

* Lo que hace el loco á la postre, hace sabio al principio.

vantage as well as grace of an earlier compliance has passed away. The nine precious volumes have shrunk to six, and these dwindled to three, while yet the like price is demanded for the few as for the many; for the remnant now as would once have made all our own.

I have already, in a former lecture, adduced a proverb which warns against a bad book as the worst of all robbers. In respect, too, of books which are not bad—nay, of which the main staple is good, but in which there is yet an admixture of evil, as is the case with so many that have come down to us from that old world not as yet partaker of Christ—there is a proverb, which may very profitably accompany us in our study of all these: *Where the bee sucks honey, the spider sucks poison.* Very profitably may this word be kept in mind by such as at any time are making themselves familiar with the classical literature of antiquity, the great writers of heathen Greece and Rome. How much of noble, how much of elevating, what love of country, what zeal for wisdom, may be drawn from them: yea, even to us Christians, what intellectual, what moral gains will they yield! Let the student be as the bee looking for honey, and from the fields and gardens of classical literature he may store it abundantly in his hive. And yet from this same body of literature what poison is it possible to draw; what loss, through familiarity with evil, of all vigorous abhorrence of it, till even the foulest enormities shall come to be regarded with a speculative curiosity rather than with an earnest hatred! yea, what lasting defilement of the imagination and the heart, may be contracted hence, till nothing shall be pure, the very mind and conscience being defiled. Let there come one whose sympathies and affinities are with the poison, and not with the honey; and in these fields it will not be impossible for him to find deadly flowers and weeds from which he may suck poison enough.

And here is one with an insight at once subtle and profound into the heart of man, *Ill-doers are ill-deemers;* and instead of any commentary on this of my own, let me quote some words which were not intended to be a commentary upon it at all, and which furnish, notwithstanding, a better than any which I could hope to give. They are words of a great English divine of the seventeenth century, who is accounting for the offence which the Pharisee took at the Lord's acceptance of the affectionate homage and costly offering of the woman that was a sinner: "Which familiar and affectionate officiousness, and sumptuous cost, together with that sinister fame that woman was noted with, could not but give much scandal to the Pharisees there present. For that dispensation of the law under which they lived making nothing perfect, but only curbing the outward actions of men; it might very well be that they, being conscious to themselves of no better motions within than of either bitterness or lust, how fair soever they carried without, could not deem Christ's acceptance of so familiar and affectionate a service from a woman of that fame to proceed from anything better than some loose and vain principle.... for by how much every one is himself obnoxious to temptation, by so much more suspicious he is that others transgress, when there is anything that may tempt out the corruptions of a man."*

With a few remarks on one proverb more, I will bring this lecture to an end. It is this: *Better a diamond with a flaw, than a pebble without one.* Here, to my mind, is the assertion of a great Christian truth, and of one which reaches deep down to the very foundations of Christian morality, the more valuable as coming to us from a people—the Chinese—beyond the range and reach of the influences of direct revelation. We may not be all aware of the many and malignant assaults which were made on the Christian faith, and on the morality of the Bible, through the character of David, by the blind and self-righteous deists of a century or more ago. Taking the scripture testimony about

* Henry More, *On Godliness*, b. 8. How remarkable a confirmation of the fact asserted in that proverb and in this passage, lies in the uses of the Greek word κακοήθεια; having, for its first meaning, an evil disposition in a man's self, it has for its second an interpreting on his part for the worst of all the actions of other men.

him, that he was the man after God's heart, and putting beside this the record of those great sins which he committed, they sought to set these great yet still isolated offences in the most hateful light; and thus to bring at once him, and those who praised him, to a common shame. But all this while, with the question of *the man*, what he was—with this, with the moral sum total of his life, to which alone the scripture testimony bore witness, and to which alone it was pledged—they concerned themselves not at all: which yet was a far more important question than what any of his single acts may have been, and that which, in the estimate of his character, was really at issue. To this question *we* answer, *a diamond*, which, if a diamond *with a flaw*, as are all but the one "whole and perfect chrysolite," would yet outvalue a mountain of *pebbles without one*, such as they were; even assuming the pebbles to *be* without, and not merely to *seem* so, because their flaw was an all-pervading one, and only not so quickly detected, inasmuch as the contrast was wanting of any clearer material which should at once reveal its presence.

LECTURE VI.

THE THEOLOGY OF PROVERBS.

I SOUGHT, as best I could, in my last lecture, to enable you to estimate the ethical worth of proverbs. Their theology alone remains; the aspects, that is, under which they contemplate, not now any more man's relations with his fellow-man, but those on which in the end all other must depend, his relations with God. Between the subject-matter, indeed, of that lecture and of this, I have found it nearly impossible to draw any accurate line of distinction. Much which was there might nearly as fitly have been here; some which I have reserved for this might already have found its place there. It is this, however, which I propose more directly to consider, namely, what proverbs have to say concerning the moral government of the world, and, more important still, concerning its Governor? How does all this present itself to the popular mind and conscience, as attested by these? What, in short, is their theology? for such, good or bad, it is evident that abundantly they have.

Here, as everywhere else, their testimony is a

mingled one. The darkness, the error, the confusion of man's heart, out of which he oftentimes sees distortedly, and sometimes sees not at all, have all embodied themselves in his word. Yet still, as it is the very nature of the false, in its separate manifestations, to resolve into nothingness, though only to be succeeded by new births in a like kind, while the true abides and continues, it has thus come to pass that we have generally in these utterances on which the stamp of permanence has been set, the nobler voices, the truer faith of humanity, in respect of its own destinies and of him by whom those destinies are ordered.

I would not hesitate to say that the great glory of proverbs in this their highest aspect, and that which makes many of them so full of blessing to those who cordially accept them, is the conviction of which they are full, that, despite all appearances to the contrary, this world is God's world, and not the world of the devil or of those wicked men who may be prospering for their hour; their faith that in the long run it will approve itself to be such: which being so, that it must be well in the end with the doer of the right, the speaker of the truth; no blind "whirligig of time," but the hand of the living God, in due time "bringing round its revenges." It is impossible to estimate too highly their bold and clear proclamation of this conviction; for it is, after all, the belief of this or the denial of this, on which everything in the life of each one of us turns; on this depends whether we shall separate ourselves from the world's falsehood and evil, and do vigorous battle against them; or acquiesce in, and be ourselves absorbed by, them.

Listen to proverbs such as these; surely they are penetrated with the assurance that one who, himself being the truth, will make truth in small and in great to triumph at the last, is ruling over all. And first, hear a proverb of our own: *A lie has no legs;* it is one true alike in its humblest application and its highest; be the lie the miserable petty falsehood which disturbs a family or a neighborhood for a day; or one of the larger frauds, the falsehoods not in word only but in act, to which a longer date and a far larger sphere is assigned, which for a time seem to fill the world, and to carry everything in triumph before them. Still the lie, in that it is a lie, always carries within itself the germs of its own dissolution. It is sure to destroy itself at last. Its priests may prop it up from without, may set it on its feet again after it has once fallen before the presence of the truth, yet this all will be labor in vain; it will only be, like Dagon, again to fall, and more shamefully and more irretrievably than before.* On the other hand, the

* Perhaps the Spanish form of this proverb is still better: La mentira tiene *cortas* las piernas; for the lie does go, though not far. Compare the French: La vérité, comme l'huile, vient audessus.

vivacity of the truth, as contrasted with this short-lived character of the lie, is well expressed in a Swiss proverb: *It takes a good many shovelfuls of earth to bury the truth.* For, bury it as deep as men may, it will have a resurrection notwithstanding. They may roll a great stone, and seal the sepulchre in which it is laid, and set a watch upon it, yet still, like its Lord, it comes forth again at its appointed hour. It can not die, being of an immortal race; for, as the Spanish proverb nobly declares, *The truth is daughter of God.**

Again, consider this proverb: *Tell the truth, and shame the devil.* It is one which will well repay a few thoughtful moments bestowed on it, and the more so, because, even while we instinctively feel its truth, the deep moral basis on which it rests may yet not reveal itself to us at once. Nay, the saying may seem to contradict the actual experience of things; for how often telling the truth—confessing, that is, some great fault, taking home to ourselves, it may be, some grievous sin—would appear anything rather than shaming the devil; shaming indeed ourselves, but rather bringing glory to him, whose glory, such as it is, is in the sin and shame of men. And yet the word is true, and deeply true, notwithstanding. The element of lies is that in which alone he who is "the father of them" lives and thrives. So long then as a wrong-doer presents

* La verdad es hija de Dios.

to himself, or seeks to present to others, the actual facts of his conduct different from what they really are, conceals, palliates, denies them, so long, in regard of that man, Satan's kingdom stands. But so soon as the things concerning himself are seen and owned by a man as they indeed exist in God's sight, as they are when weighed in the balances of the eternal righteousness; when once a man has brought himself to tell the truth to himself, and, where need requires, to others also, then having done, and in so far as he has done this, he has abandoned the devil's standard, he belongs to the kingdom of the truth; and as belonging to it he may rebuke, and does rebuke and put to shame, all makers and lovers of a lie, even to the very prince of them all. "Give glory to God," was what Joshua said to Achan, when he would lead him to confess his guilt. This is but the other and fairer side of the tapestry; this is but *shame the devil*, on its more blessed side.

Once more;—the Latin proverb, *The voice of the people, the voice of God*,* is one which it is well worth our while to understand. If it were affirmed in this that every outcry of the multitude, supposing only it be loud enough and wide enough, ought to be accepted as the voice of God speaking through them, no proposition more foolish or more impious could well be imagined. But *the voice of*

* Vox populi, vox Dei.

the people is something very different from this. The proverb rests on the assumption that the foundations of man's being are laid in the truth; from which it will follow, that no conviction which is really a conviction of the universal humanity, but reposes on a true ground: no faith, which is indeed the faith of mankind, but has a reality corresponding to it; for, as Jeremy Taylor has said, "it is not a vain noise, when many nations join their voices in the attestation or detestation of an action." The task and difficulty, of course, must ever be to discover what this faith and what these convictions are; and this can only be done by an induction from a sufficient number of facts, and in sufficiently different times, to enable us to feel confident that we have indeed seized that which is the constant quantity of truth in them all, and separated this from the inconstant one of falsehood and error, evermore offering itself in its room; that we have not taken some momentary cry, wrung out by interest, by passion, or by pain, for *the voice of God;* but claimed this august title only for that true voice of humanity, which, unless everything be false, we have a right to assume an echo of the voice of God.

Thus, to take an example, the natural horror everywhere felt in regard of marriages contracted between those very near in blood, has been always and with right appealed to as a potent argument against such marriages. The induction is so large, that is, the nations who have agreed in entertaining this horror are so many, oftentimes nations disagreeing in almost everything besides — the times during which this instinctive revolt against such unions has been felt, extend through such long ages — that the few exceptions, even where they are of civilized nations, as of the Egyptians who married their sisters, or of the Persians, among whom marriages more dreadful still were allowed, and with yet better reason the exception of any savage tribes in whom the true humanity had disappeared, can not be allowed any weight. They can not only be regarded as violations of the divine order of man's life; not as evidences that we have falsely imagined an order where there was none. Here is a true *voice of the people;* and on the grounds laid down above, we have a right to assume this to be a *voice of God* as well. And so too, with respect to the existence of a First Cause, Creator and Upholder of all things, the universal consent and conviction of all people, the *consensus gentium*, must be considered of itself a mighty evidence in its favor; a testimony which God is pleased to render to himself through his creatures. This man or that, this generation or the other, might be deceived, but all men and all generations could not; the *vox populi* makes itself felt as a *vox Dei.* The existence here and there of an atheist no more disturbs our conclusion that it is of the essence of man's nature to believe in a God, than do such monstrous births as from time to time find place, children with two heads or with no arms, shake our assurance that it is the normal condition of man to have one head and two arms.

This last is one of the proverbs which may be said to belong to the Apology for Natural Religion. There are others, of which it would not be far-fetched to affirm that they belong to the Apology for Revealed. Thus it was very usual with Voltaire and other infidels of his time to appeal to the present barrenness and desolation of Palestine, in proof that it could never have supported the vast population which the Scripture everywhere assumes or affirms. A proverb in the language of the arch-scoffer himself might, if he had given heed to it, have put him on the right track, had he wished to be put upon it, for understanding how this could have been: *As the man is worth, his land is worth.** Man is lord of his outward condition to a far greater extent than is commonly assumed; even climate which seems at first sight so completely out of his reach, it is his immensely to modify; and if Nature stamps herself on him, he stamps himself yet more powerfully on Nature.

It is not a mere figure of speech, that of the psalmist, "A fruitful land maketh he barren for the wickedness of them that dwell therein." (Ps. cvii. 34.)

* Tant vaut l'homme, tant vaut sa terre.

God makes it barren, and ever less capable of nourishing its inhabitants; but he makes it so through the sloth, the indolence, the short-sightedness of those that should have dressed and kept it. In the condition of a land may be found the echo, the reflection, the transcript of the moral and spiritual condition of those that should cultivate it; where one is waste, the other will be waste also. Under the desolating curse of Mohammedan domination the fairest portions of the earth have gone back from a garden to a wilderness: but only let that people for whom Palestine is yet destined return to it again, and return a righteous nation, and in a little while all the descriptions of its earlier fertility will be more than borne out by its later, and it will easily sustain its millions again.

How many proverbs, which can not be affirmed to have been originally made for the kingdom of heaven, do yet in their highest fulfilment manifestly belong to it, so that it seems as of right to claim that for its own, even as it claims, or rather reclaims, whatever else is good or true in the world, the seeds of truth wherever dispersed abroad, as belonging rightfully to itself. Thus there is that beautiful proverb, of which Pythagoras is reputed the author, *The things of friends are in common.** Where does this find its exhaustive fulfilment, but in the

* Κοινὰ τὰ τῶν φίλων.

communion of saints, their communion not with one another merely, though indeed this is a part of its fulfilment, but in their communion with him who is the friend of all good men? That such a conclusion lay legitimately in the words Socrates plainly saw; who argued from it, that since good men were the friends of the gods, therefore whatever things were the gods' were also theirs; being, when he thus concluded, as near as one who had not the highest light of all, could be to that great word of the apostle's, "All things are yours."

Nor can I otherwise than esteem the ancient proverb as a very fine one, and one which we may gladly claim for our own, *Many meet the gods, but few salute them.* How often do *the gods* (for I will keep in the language which this proverb suggests and supplies) *meet* men in the shape of a sorrow which might be a purifying one, of a joy which might elevate their hearts to thankfulness and praise; in a sickness or a recovery, a disappointment or a success; and yet how few, as it must be sadly owned, *salute* them—how few recognise their august presences in this joy or this sorrow, this blessing added or this blessing taken away! As this proverb has reference to men's failing to *see* the Divine presences, so let me observe, by the way, there is a very grand French one which expresses the same truth, under the image of a failing to *hear* the Divine voices, those voices being drowned by the deafening hubbub of the world: *The noise is so great, one can not hear God thunder.**

Here is another proverb which the church has long since claimed, at least in its import, for her own: *One man, no man.*† I should find it very hard indeed to persuade myself that whoever uttered it first, attached to it no deeper meaning than Erasmus gives him credit for— namely, that nothing important can be effected by a single man, destitute of the help of his fellows.‡ The word is a far more profound one than this, and rests on that great truth upon which the deeper thinkers of antiquity laid so much stress—namely, that *in the idea* the state precedes the individual, man not being merely accidentally *gregarious*, but essentially *social*. The solitary man, it would say, is a monstrous conception, so utterly maimed and crippled must he be; the condition of solitariness involving so entire a suppression of all which belongs to the development of that wherein the true idea of humanity resides, of all which differences man from the beasts of the field; and in this sense *One man* is *no man;* and this, I am sure, the proverb from the first intended. Nor may we stop here. This word is capable of, and seems to demand, a still higher application to man, as a destined member of the kingdom of

* Le bruit est si fort, qu'on n'entend pas Dieu tonner.

† Εἷς ἀνὴρ, οὐδεὶς ἀνήρ.

‡ Sensus est nihil egregium præstari posse ab uno homine, omni auxilio destituto.

Heaven. But he can only be in training for this, when he is, and regards himself, as not alone, but the member of a family. As *one man* he is *no man;* and the strength and value of what is called church teaching is greatly this, that it does recognise and realize this fact, that it contemplates and deals with the faithful man, not as isolated, but as one of an organic body, with duties which flow as moral necessities from his position therein; rather than by himself, and as one whose duties to others are indeed only the exercise of private graces for his own benefit. And all that are called church doctrines, when they really understand themselves, have their root and their real strength in that great truth which this proverb declares, that *One man is no man*, that only in a fellowship and communion is or can any man be aught.

And then there is another proverb, which Plato so loved to quote against the sophists, the men who flattered and corrupted the nobler youth of Athens, promising to impart to them easy short cuts to the attainment of wisdom and knowledge and philosophy; and this, without demanding the exercise of any labor or patience or self-denial on their parts. But with the proverb, *Good things are hard*,* he continually rebuked their empty pretensions; with this he made at least suspicious their promises; and this proverb, true in the sense where-

* Χαλεπὰ τὰ καλά.

in Plato used it—and that sense was earnest and serious enough—yet surely reappears, glorified and transfigured, but recognisable still, in the Savior's words: "The kingdom of heaven is taken by violence, and the violent take it by force."

This method of looking in proverbs for a higher meaning than any which lies on their surface, or which they seem to bear on their fronts—or rather of searching out their highest intention, and claiming that as their truest, even though it should not be that seen in them by most, or that which lay nearest to them at their first generation—is one that will lead us in many interesting paths. And it is not merely those of heathen antiquity which shall thus be persuaded often, and that without any forcing, to render up a Christian meaning; but (as was indeed to be expected) still more often those of a later time, even those which the world had seemed to claim for its own, shall be found to move in a spiritual sphere as their truest. Let me offer in evidence of this these four or five, which come to us from Italy: *He who has love in his heart, has spurs in his sides.—Love rules without law.—Love rules his kingdom without a sword.—Love knows nothing of labor.—Love is the master of all arts.** Take these, even with the necessary drawbacks of

* Chi ha l'amor nel petto, ha lo sprone a i fianchi.—Amor regge senza legge. (Cf. Rom. xiii. 9, 10.)—Amor regge il suo regno senza spada.—Amor non conosce travaglio. (Cf. Gen. xxix. 20, 30.)—Di tutte le arti maestro è amore.

my English translation, but still more in their original beauty; and how exquisitely do they set forth, in whatever light you regard them, the free creative impulses of love, its delight to labor and to serve; how worthily do they glorify the kingdom of love as the only kingdom of a free and joyful obedience. While yet at the same time, if we would appreciate them at *all* their worth, is it possible to stop short of an application of them to that kingdom of love, which, because it is in the highest sense such, is is also a kingdom of heaven? And then, what precious witness do these utterances contain, the more precious as current among a people nursed in the theology of Rome, against the shameless assertion that selfishness is the only motive sufficient to produce good (?) works: for in such an assertion the Romish impugners of a free justification constantly deal, charging this which we hold, of our justification by faith only, which when translated into the language of ethics is at least as important in the province of morality as it is in that of faith, with being an immoral doctrine, and not so fruitful in deeds of love as one which should connect these deeds with a selfish thought of promoting our own safety thereby.

There are proverbs which reach the height of evangelical morality. "Little gospels"* the Spaniard has somewhat too boldly entitled his; yet are

* Evangelios pequeños.

there certainly many which at once we feel could nowhere have arisen or obtained their circulation but under the influence of Christian faith, being in spirit, and often in form as well as in spirit, the outbirths of it. Thus is it with that exquisitely beautiful proverb of our own, *The way to heaven is by Weeping-Cross;** nor otherwise with the Spanish, *God never wounds with both hands*†—not with *both*, for he ever reserves one with which to bind up and to heal. And another Spanish, evidently intended to give the sum and substance of all which in life is to be desired the most, *Peace and patience, and death with penitence*,‡ gives this sum certainly only as it presents itself to the Christian eye. And this of ours is Christian both in form and in spirit: *Every cross hath its inscription*—the name, that is, inscribed upon it, of the person for whom it was shaped. It was intended for those shoulders upon which it is laid, and will adapt itself to them: that fearful word is never true which a spirit greatly vexed spake in the hour of its impatience: "I have little faith in the paternal love which I need; so ruthless or so negligent seems the government of this earth."§

* Der Weg zum Himmel geht durch Kreuzdorn. Compare the medieval obverse of the same: Via Crucis, via lucis.

† No hiere Dios con dos manos.

‡ Paz y paciencia, y muerte con penitencia.

§ *Memoirs of Margaret Fuller*, vol. 3, p. 266. In respect of words like these, wrung out from moments of agony, and not the abiding convictions of the utterer, may we not venture to hope that our own

So too is it with that ancient German proverb, *When God loathes aught, men presently loathe it too.** He who first uttered this must have been one who had watched long the ways by which shame and honor travel in this world; and, in this watching, must have noted how it ever came to pass that even worldly honor tarried not long with them from whom the true honor which cometh from God had departed. For the worldly honor is but a shadow and reflex that waits upon the heavenly; it may indeed linger for a little, but it will be only for a little, after it is divorced from its substance. Where the honor from him has been withdrawn, he causes in one way or another the honor from men, ere long, to be withdrawn too. When he loathes, presently man loathes also. The saltless salt is not merely cast out by him, but is trodden under foot *of men* (Matt. v. 13). A Louis the Fifteenth's death-bed is, in its way, as hideous to the natural as it is to the spiritual eye.†

It would be interesting to collect, as with reverence one might, variations on scriptural proverbs or sayings, which the proverbs of this world supply:

proverb, *For mad words deaf ears*, is often graciously true, even in the very courts of heaven?

* Wenn Gott ein Ding verdreufst, so verdreufst es auch bald die Menschen.

† The following have all a right to be termed Christian proverbs: Chi non vuol servir ad un solo Signor, à molti ha da servir; — E padron del mondo chi lo disprezza, schiavo chi lo apprezza; — Quando Dios quiere, con todos vientos llueve.

and this, both in those cases where the latter have grown out of the former, owing more nearly or more remotely their existence to them, and in those also where they are independent of them—so far, that is, as anything true can be independent of the absolute truth. Some of those which follow evidently belong to one of these classes, some to the other. Thus Solomon has said, "It is better to dwell in the corner of the housetop than with a brawling woman in a wide house" (Prov. xxi. 9); and again, "Better a dry morsel and quietness therewith, than a house full of sacrifices with strife" (Prov. xvii. 1). With these compare the two proverbs, a Latin and a Spanish, adduced below.* The psalmist has said, "As he loved cursing, so let it come unto him" (Ps. cix. 17). The Turks express their faith in this same law of the divine retaliations: *Curses, like chickens, always come home to roost;* they return, that is, to those from whom they went forth. In the Yoruba language there is a proverb to the same effect, *Ashes always fly back in the face of him that throws them;* while our own, *Harm watch, harm catch*, and the Spanish, *Who sows thorns, let him not go unshod*,† are utterances of very nearly the same conviction. Our Lord declares, that without his Father there falls

† Non quam late sed quam læte habites, refert.—Mas vale un pedazo de pan con amor, que gallinas con dolor.

* Quien siembra abrojos, no ande descalzo. Compare the Latin: Si vultur es, cadaver expecta.

no single sparrow to the ground, that "not one of them is forgotten before God" (Luke xii. 6). The same truth of a *providentia specialissima* (between which and no providence at all there is indeed no tenable position) is asserted in the Catalan proverb, *No leaf moves but God wills it.** Again, he has said, "No man can serve two masters" (Matt. vi. 24). And the Spanish proverb, *He who has to serve two masters, has to lie to one.*† Or compare with Matt. xix. 29, this remarkable Arabic proverb, *Purchase the next world with this, so shalt thou win both.* He has spoken of "mammon of unrighteousness;" indicating thereby, in Leighton's words, that "iniquity is so involved in the notion of riches, that it can very hardly be separated from them;" and this phrase Jerome illustrates by a proverb that would not otherwise have reached us: "That saying," he says, "appears true to me: *A rich man is either himself an unjust one, or the heir of one.*"‡ Again, the Lord has said, "Many be called, but few chosen" (Matt. xx. 16); many have the outward marks of a Christian profession, few the inner substance. Some early fathers loved much to bring

* No se mou la fulla, que Deu no ha vulla. This is one of the proverbs of which the peculiar grace and charm nearly disappears in the rendering.

† Quien à dos señores ha de servir, al uno ha de mentir.

‡ Verum mihi videtur illud: Dives aut iniquus, aut iniqui hæres. Out of a sense of the same, as I take it, the striking Italian proverb had its rise: Mai diventò fiume grande, chi non v'entrasse acqua torbida.

into comparison with this a Greek proverb, spoken indeed quite independently of it, and long previously, and the parallel certainly is a singularly happy one: *the thyrsus-bearers are many, but the bacchants few;** many assume the signs and outward tokens of inspiration, whirling the thyrsus aloft; but those whom the god indeed fills with his spirit are few all the while.†

It has been sometimes a matter of consideration to me whether we of the clergy might not make larger use, though of course it would be only occasional, of proverbs in our public teaching than we do. Great popular preachers of time past—or, seeing that this phrase has now so questionable a sound, great preachers for the people, such as have found their way to the universal heart of their fellows, addressing themselves not to that which some men had different from others, but to that rather which each had in common with all—have been ever

* Πολλοί τοι ναρθηκοφόροι, παῦροι δέ τε βάκχοι.

† The fact which this proverb proclaims, of a great gulf existing between what men profess and what they are, is one too frequently repeating itself and thrusting itself on the notice of all, not to have found its utterance in an infinite variety of forms, although none perhaps so deep and poetical as this. Thus there is another Greek line, fairly represented by this Latin:—

Qui tauros stimulent multi, sed rarus arator;

and there is the classical Roman proverb: Non omnes qui habent citharam, sunt citharœdi; and the medieval rhyming verse:—

Non est venator quivis per cornua flator;

and this Eastern word: *Hast thou mounted the pulpit, thou art not therefore a preacher;* with many more.

great employers of proverbs. Thus he who would know the riches of those in the German tongue, with the vigorous manifold employment of which they are capable, will find no richer mine to dig in than the works of Luther. And such employment of them would, I believe, with our country congregations, be especially valuable. Any one, who by after investigation has sought to discover how much our rustic hearers carry away even from the sermons to which they have attentively listened, will find that it is hardly ever the course and tenor of the argument, supposing the discourse to have contained such; but if anything was uttered, as it used so often to be by the best puritan preachers, tersely, pointedly, epigrammatically, this will have stayed by them, while all beside has gone. Now, the merits of terseness and point, which have caused other words to be remembered, are exactly those which signalize the proverb, and generally in a yet higher degree.

It need scarcely be observed, that, if thus used, they will have to be employed with prudence and discretion, and with a careful selection. Thus, even with the example of so grave a divine as Bishop Sanderson, I should hesitate to employ in a sermon such a proverb as *Over shoes, over boots*—one which he declares to be the motto of some, who having advanced a certain way in sin, presently become utterly wretchless, caring not, and counting it indifferent how much further they advance. Nor would I exactly recommend such use of a proverb as St. Bernard makes, who, in a sermon on the angels, desiring to show, *à priori*, the extreme probability of their active and loving ministries in the service of men, adduces the Latin proverb, *Who loves me, loves my dog;** and proceeds to argue thus: We are the dogs under Christ's table; the angels love him, they therefore love us.

But, although not exactly thus, the thing, I am persuaded, might be done, and with profit. Thus, in a discourse warning against sins of the tongue, there are many words which we might produce of our own to describe the mischief it inflicts, that would be flatter, duller, less likely to be remembered than the old proverb, *The tongue is not steel, but it cuts.* On God's faithfulness in sustaining, upholding, rewarding his servants, there are feebler things which we might bring out of our own treasure-house, than to remind our hearers of that word, *He who serves God, serves a good Master.* And this one might sink deep, telling of the enemy whom every one of us has the most to fear: *No man has a worse friend than he brings with him from home.* It stands in striking agreement with Augustine's remarkable prayer, "Deliver me from

* Qui me amat, amat et canem meum. (*In Fest. S. Mich., Serm.* 1, § 3.)

the evil man, from myself."* Or again, *Ill weeds grow apace;* with how lively an image does this set forth to us the rank, luxuriant up-growth of sinful lusts and desires in the garden of an uncared-for, untended heart. I know not whether we might presume sufficient quickness of apprehension on the part of our hearers to venture on the following: *The horse which draws its halter is not quite escaped;* but I can hardly imagine a happier illustration of the fact, that so long as any remnant of a sinful habit is retained by us, so long as we draw this halter, we make but an idle boast of our liberty; we may, by aid of that which we still drag with us, be at any moment again entangled altogether in the bondage, from which we seemed to have entirely escaped.

In every language, some of its noblest proverbs, such as oftentimes are admirably adapted for this application of which I am speaking, are those embodying men's confidence in God's moral government of the world, in his avenging righteousness, however much there may be in the confusions of the present evil time to provoke a doubt or even a denial of this. Thus, *Punishment is lame, but it comes*—which, if not old, yet rests on an image derived from antiquity—is good; although inferior in every way, in energy of expression as in fulness of sense, to the ancient Greek one: *The mill of*

* Libera me ab homine malo, a meipso.

God grinds late, but grinds to powder;[*] for this brings in the further thought, that his judgments, however long they tarry, yet when they arrive are crushing ones. There is, indeed, another of our own, not unworthy to be set beside this, announcing, though with quite another image, the same fact of the tardy but terrible arrivals of judgment: *God comes with leaden feet, but strikes with iron hands.* And then, how awfully sublime another which has come down to us as part of the wisdom of the ancient heathen world; I mean the following: *The feet of the (avenging) deities are shod with wool.*[†] Here a new thought is introduced: the noiseless approach and advance of these judgments, as noiseless as the steps of one whose feet were wrapped in wool—the manner in which they overtake secure sinners even in the hour of their utmost security. Who that has studied the history of the great crimes and criminals of the world, but will with a shuddering awe set his seal to the truth of this proverb? Indeed, meditating on such and on the source from which we have derived them, one is sometimes tempted to believe that the faith in a Divine retribution evermore making itself felt in the world, this sense of a Nemesis, as men used to

* Ὀψὲ θεῶν ἀλέουσι μύλοι, ἀλέουσι δὲ λεπτά.

We may compare the Latin: Habet Deus suas horas, et moras; and the Spanish: Dios no se queja, mas lo suyo no lo deja.

† Dii laneos habent pedes.

call it, was stronger and deeper in the earlier and better days of heathendom, than alas! it is in a sunken Christendom now.

But to resume. Even those proverbs which have acquired a use which seems to unite at once the trivial and the profane, may yet, on closer inspection, be found to be very far from having either triviality or profaneness cleaving to them. There is one, for instance, often taken lightly enough upon the lips, *Talk of the devil, and he is sure to appear;* or, as it used to be, *Talk of the devil, and his imps will appear;* or, as in German it is, *Paint the devil on the wall, and he will show himself anon:* which yet contains truth serious and important enough, if we would only give heed to it; it contains, in fact, a very solemn warning against a very dangerous sin—I mean, curiosity about evil. It has been often noticed, and is a very curious psychological fact, that there is a tendency in a great crime to reproduce itself—to call forth, that is, other crimes of the same character: and there is a fearful response which the evil we may hear or read about, is in danger of finding in our own hearts. This danger, then, assuredly makes it true wisdom and a piece of moral prudence, on the part of all to whom this is permitted, to avoid knowing or learning about the evil; especially when neither duty nor necessity oblige them thereto. It is men's wisdom to talk as little about the devil, either with themselves or with others, as they can, lest he appear to them. "I agree with you," says Niebuhr very profoundly in one of his letters,* "that it is better not to read books in which you make the acquaintance of the devil." And certainly there is a remarkable commentary on this proverb, so interpreted, in the earnest warning given to the children of Israel, that they should not so much as *inquire* how the nations which were before them in Canaan, served their gods, with what cruelties, with what abominable impurities, lest through this inquiry they should be themselves entangled in the same (Deut. xii. 29, 30). They were not to talk about the devil, lest he should appear to them.

And other proverbs, too, which at first sight may seem over-familiar with the name of the great enemy of mankind, yet contain lessons which it would be an infinite pity to lose; as this German, *Where the devil can not come, he will send;*† a proverb of very serious import, which excellently sets out to us the *penetrative* character of temptations, and the certainty that they will follow and find men out in their secretest retreats. It rebukes the absurdity of supposing that by any outward arrangements, cloistral retirements, flights into the wilderness, sin can be kept at a distance. So far

* *Life*, vol. i., p. 312.

† Wo der Teufel nicht hin mag kommen, da send er seinen Boten hin.

from this, temptations will inevitably overleap all these outward and merely artificial barriers which may be raised up against them; for our great enemy is as formidable from a seeming distance as in close combat; *where he can not come, he will send.* There are others of the same family, as the following: *The devil's meal is half bran*—or *all bran*, as the Italians still more boldly proclaim it;* unrighteous gains are sure to disappoint the getter; the pleasures of sin, even in this present time, are largely dashed with its pains. And this, *He had need of a long spoon that eats with the devil;* men fancy they can cheat the arch-cheater, can advance in partnership with him up to a certain point, and then, whenever the connection becomes too dangerous, break it off at their will; being sure in this to be miserably deceived. Granting these and the like to have been often carelessly uttered, yet they all rest upon a true moral basis in the main.

I have adduced in the course of these lectures no inconsiderable number of proverbs, and have sought for the most part to draw from them lessons, which were lessons in common for us all. There is one, however, which I must not pass over, for I feel that it contains an especial lesson for myself, and a lesson which I should do wisely and well, at this present time, to lay to heart. When the Spaniards would describe a tedious writer, one who

* La farina del diavolo se ne và in semola.

possesses the art of exhausting the patience of his readers, they say of him, *He leaves nothing in his inkstand.* The phrase is a singularly happy one; for assuredly there is no such secret of tediousness, no such certain means of wearing out the attention of our readers or our hearers, as the attempt to say everything ourselves, instead of leaving something to be filled up by their intelligence; while the merits of a composition are often displayed as really, if not so prominently, in what is passed over as in what is set down; in nothing more than in the just measure of the confidence which it shows in the capacities and powers of those to whom it is addressed. I would not willingly come under the condemnation which waits on them who thus *leave nothing in their inkstand;* and, lest I should do so, I will bring now this my final lecture to its close, and ask you to draw out for yourselves those further lessons from proverbs, which I am sure they are abundantly capable of yielding.

APPENDIX.

ON THE METRICAL LATIN PROVERBS OF THE MIDDLE AGES. (See p. 37.)

I HAVE not seen anywhere brought together a collection of these medieval proverbs cast into the form of a rhyming hexameter. Erasmus, though he often illustrates the proverbs of the ancient world by those of the new, does not quote, as far as I am aware, through the whole of his enormous collection, a single one of these which occupy a middle place between the two; a fact which in its way is curiously illustrative of the degree to which the attention of the great Humanists, at the revival of learning, was exclusively directed to the classical literature of Greece and Rome. Yet proverbs in this form exist in considerable number; being of very various degrees of merit, as will be seen from the following selection; in which some are keen and piquant enough, while others are of very subordinate value; those which seemed to me utterly valueless —and they were not few—I have excluded altogether. the reader familiar with proverbs, will detect correspondents to very many of them, besides the few which I have quoted, in one modern language or another, often in many.

Accipe, sume, cape, tria sunt gratissima Papæ.

Let me observe here, once for all, that the lengthening of the final syllable in *capē*, is not to be set down to the ignorance or carelessness of the writer; but in the theory of the medieval hexameter, the unavoidable stress or pause on the first syllable of the third foot was counted sufficient to lengthen the shortest syllable in that position.

Ad secreta poli curas extendere noli.
Ægro sanato, frustra dices, Numerato.
Amphora sub veste raro portatur honeste.
Ante Dei vultum nihil unquam restat inultum.
Ante molam primus qui venit, non molat imus.

A rule of natural equity: Prior tempore, prior jure; *First come, first serve.* — "Whoso first cometh to the mill, first grint." — *Chaucer.*

Arbor naturam dat fructibus atque figuram.
Arbor ut ex fructu, sic nequam noscitur actu.
Ars compensabit quod vis tibi magna negabit.
Artem natura superat sine vi, sine curâ.
Aspera vox, Ite, sed vox est blanda, Venite.

An allus'on to Matt. xxv. 34, 41.

Cari rixantur, rixantes conciliantur.
Carius est carum, si prægustatur amarum.
Casus dementis correctio fit sapientis.
Catus sæpe satur cum capto mure jocatur.
Cautus homo cavit, si quem natura notavit.
Conjugium sine prole, dies veluti sine sole.
Contra vim mortis non herbula crescit in hortis.
Cui puer assuescit, major dimittere nescit.

The same appears also in a pentameter, and under an Horatian image: Quod nova testa capit, inveterata sapit.

Cum jocus est verus, jocus est malus atque severus.

So the Spanish: Malas son las burlas verdaderas.

Curvum se præbet quod in uncum crescere debet.
Curia Romana non quærit ovem sine lanâ.
Dat bene, dat multum, qui dat cum munere vultum.

"He that showeth mercy, with cheerfulness." (Rom. xii. 8.) Cf. Ecclus. xxxv. 9; SENECA, *De Benef.*, i. 1.

Deficit ambobus qui vult servire duobus.
Dormit secure, cui non est functio curæ.

Far from court, far from care.

Ebibe vas totum, si vis cognoscere potum.
Est facies testis, quales intrinsecus estis.
Est nulli certum cui pugna velit dare sertum.
Ex linguâ stultâ veniunt incommoda multa.
Ex minimo crescit, sed non cito fama quiescit.
Fœmina ridendo flendo fallitque canendo.
Frangitur ira gravis, cum fit responsio suavis.
Fures in lite pandunt abscondita vitæ.

So in Spanish: Riñen les comrades, y dicense las verdades.

Furtivus potus plenus dulcedine totus.
Hoc retine verbum, frangit Deus omne superbum.
Illa mihi patria est, ubi pascor, non ubi nascor.
Impedit omne forum defectus denariorum.
In vestimentis non stat sapientia mentis.
In vili veste nemo tractatur honeste.

The Russians have a worthier proverb: *A man's reception is according to his coat; his dismissal according to his sense.*

Linguam frænare plus est quam castra domare.
Lingua susurronis est pejor felle draconis.
Musca, canes, mimi veniunt ad fercula primi.
Mus salit in stratum, cum scit non adfore catum.
Ne credas undam, placidam non esse profundam.
Nil cito mutabis, donec meliora parabis.
Nobilitas morum plus ornat quam genitorum.
Non colit arva bene, qui semen mandat arenæ.
Non est in mundo dives qui dicit, Abundo.
Non habet anguillam, per caudam qui tenet illam.
Non stat securus, qui protinus est ruiturus.
Non vult scire satur quid jejunus patiatur.
Omnibus est nomen, sed idem non omnibus omen.

In a world of absolute truth, every name would be the exact utterance of the thing or person that bore it; but in our world, not every Irenæus is peaceable, nor every Blanche a blonde. Vigilantius ought rather, according to Jerome, to have been named Dormitantius; and Antiochus Epiphanes (the Illustrious), was for the Jews Antiochus Epimanes (the Insane).

Parvis imbutus tentabis grandia tutus.
Pelle sub agninâ latitat mens sæpe lupina.
Per multum, Cras, Cras, omnis, consumitur ætas.
Prodigus est natus de parco patre creatus.
Quando tumet venter, produntur facta latenter.
Qui bene vult fari, debet bene præmeditari.
Quidquid agit mundus, monachus vult esse secundus.
Qui petit alta nimis, retro lapsus ponitur imis.
Qui pingit florem non pingit floris odorem.
Qui se non noscat, vicini jurgia poscat.
Quisquis amat luscam, luscam putat esse venustam.

Quisquis amat ranam, ranam putat esse Dianam.
Quod raro cernit oculi lux, cor cito spernit.
Quo minime reris, de gurgite pisce frueris.
Quos vult sors ditat, et quos vult sub pede tritat.
Res satis est nota, plus fœtent stercora mota.
Scribatur portis, Meretrix est janua mortis.
Sepes calcatur, quâ pronior esse putatur.
Si curiam curas, pariet tibi curia curas.
Si nequeas plures, vel te solummodo cures.
Si non morderis, cane quid latrante vereris?
Stare diu nescit, quod non aliquando quiescit.
Subtrahe ligna focis, flammam restinguere si vis.
Sunt asini multi solum bino pede fulti.
Sus magis in cœno gaudet quam fonte sereno.
Tam male nil cusum, quod nullum prosit in usum.
Totâ equidem novi plus testâ pars valet ovi.
Ultra posse viri non vult Deus ulla requiri.
Verba satis celant mores, eademque revelant.
Vos inopes nostis, quis amicus quisve sit hostis.
Vulpes vult fraudem, lupus agnum, fœmina laudem.

Add to these a few of the same description, but unrhymed:—

Catus amat pisces, sed non vult tingere plantam.

It is with this proverb, which is almost of all languages, that Lady Macbeth taunts her husband, as one—

"Letting, 'I dare not,' wait upon, 'I would,'
Like the poor cat i' the adage."—Act I. Scene 7.

Cochlea consiliis, in factis esto volucris.
Dat Deus omne bonum, sed non per cornua taurum.

The Chinese say: *Even the ripest fruit does not drop into one's mouth;* and another Latin: Non volat in buccas assa columba tuas.

Ense cadunt multi, perimit sed crapula plures.
Furfure se miscens porcorum dentibus estur.

With a slight variation the Italian: Chi si fa fango, il porco lo calpesta.

Ipsa dies quandoque parens, quandoque noverca.
Invidus haud eadem semper quatit ostia Dæmon.
Mirari, non rimari, sapientia vera est.
Nomina si nescis, perit et cognitio rerum.
Non stillant omnes quas cernis in aëre nubes.
Non venit ad silvam, qui cuncta rubeta veretur.
Pro ratione Deus dispertit frigora vestis.
Quod rarum carum; vilescit quotidianum.
Sermones blandi non radunt ora loquentis.
Stultorum calami carbones, mœnia chartæ.

So the French: Muraille blanche, papier des sots.

Add further a few which occupy two lines:—

Argue consultum, te diliget; argue stultum,
Avertet vultum, nec te dimittet inultum.

Balnea cornici non prosunt, nec meretrici;
Nec meretrix munda, nec cornix alba fit undâ.

Dives eram dudum; fecerunt me tria nudum;
Alea, vina, Venus; tribus his sum factus egenus.

Quando mulcetur villanus, pejor habetur;
Ungentem pungit, pungentem rusticus ungit.

Latin medieval ones in the same spirit abound: among others this detestable one with its curious triple rhyme: Rustica gens est optima flens, et pessima ridens.

Si bene barbatum faceret sua barba beatum,
Nullus in hoc circo queat esse beatior hirco.

Si quâ sede sedes, et sit tibi commoda sedes,
Illâ sede sede, nec ab illâ sede recede.

Hoc scio pro certo, quod si cum stercore certo,
Vinco seu vincor, semper ego maculor.

Multum deliro, si cuique placere requiro;
Omnia qui potuit, hâc sine dote fuit.

Permutant mores homines, cum dantur honores;
Corde stat inflato pauper, honore dato.

THE END.

www.ingramcontent.com/pod-product-compliance
Lightning Source LLC
LaVergne TN
LVHW021401110826
845150LV00007B/1740